Tide and the Crannog

By Ryan Andrew McMahon

Text © 2012 Ryan Andrew McMahon

All rights reserved. Any reproduction of the content within is prohibited without written permission from the publisher and Author.

Orders: www.createspace.com
www.amazon.com
e-mail: tideandthecrannog@gmail.com

.... Dedicated to my family....

**Heavenly Father,
Divine Mother,
All that is,
Great Spirit,
Grand Mother,
I give thanks.**

Contents

FOREWORD 1

1 WOE AND APOPHENIA 5

2 IRIS OF THE CHILD 10

3 WITCHES AND QUEENS 19

4 THE LIGHT 35

5 LIGHT LEADS TO LOVE 47

6 TRANSCRIPTIONS 50

7 THE WITHERING 58

8 FIRST LODGE 63

9 HEART 71

10 QUESTIONS 74

11 MAN IN LOVE 79

12 DREAMING 81

13 THE HUMAN LINK TO SPIRIT 88

14 STILL LEARNING 93

15 CALVIN BROWN 95

16 TONAL, NAGUAL, TOLTEC 99

17 THE TOLTEC PATH TO FREEDOM 107

18 FAMILY AND FRIENDS 111

19 RIVER HEAD 114

20 PAIN AND CHANGE 120

21. THE FASTER YOU PURSUE YOUR SHADOW
... THE FASTER IT FLEES 127

22 ANGER 135

23 KEEPING THE ISLAND ALIVE 140

SPECIAL THANKS 148

All paintings/photos are by Ryan Andrew McMahon.

FOREWORD

by Ian Brandon McMahon

Yes, the author of this book is indeed my brother and best friend. I must admit that my younger brother has impressed me again and again from childhood to adulthood. I am fortunate enough to have a solid and loving relationship with him, which allows us to remain close and share in each other's growth through all of life's ups and downs.

Ryan was the first one to travel across the Atlantic to tour Europe at the young age of 18. A feat I was surely envious of, he came back a changed person, as his small world had suddenly expanded. He has a deep love for adventures that take him to foreign lands where he can learn, explore, and connect with both the people, and natural beauty found around the world.

He was the first person to really open my mind to the metaphysical world and ideas of abstract thought. I witnessed my brother at age 19 starting to take on heavy disciplines of daily meditation, prayer, and the reading of many spiritual texts. This was a bit surprising to me at first. He introduced me to books by Alan Watts, Paramahansa Yogananda, and Carlos Castaneda just to name a few. Over the following months and years our daily conversations were often deeply spiritual, profoundly stimulating, and very rewarding. A five minute chat could grow into an exciting two hour deep discussion on spiritual enlightenment, often leaving each other better off than before.

I saw Ryan's demeanor changing, evolving in a more positive direction. He became more mature, aware, compassionate, accepting, giving and creative. He started painting as he went through a period of inspiration and creativity. This was all sparked by a chance encounter with a clairvoyant woman named Antoinette Spurrier. After meeting her, he was forever changed, and motivated to learn more about the metaphysical world. He eventually introduced us as well. I have never been a religious

1

man, and have actually been somewhat turned off by most of my encounters with various people trying to save my soul. My thought is that no one knows for sure exactly what God is. Life is a mystery. I feel it is right to admit as a member of the humble human race, that we do not fully know or understand all there is to know. In fact, my gut has told me for a long time, that we don't know the half of it. I suspect many thousands of years from now, the people of that day may look back at us and wonder how we could have been so naive. I have gone through periods of my life questioning if God even existed. Eventually I come back to the fact that I cannot deny a higher intelligence found in all that surrounds us here on planet Earth. I also reached a point where it is okay not to know.

One day after Ryan urged me to meet Antoinette, I scheduled a visit with her at her home. She is a sweetheart of a woman, kind of like a long lost grandmother to me. She came across as very genuine and loving. I had never been to a "so called" psychic before; so I had my reservations and suspicions. Long story short is that not only did she tell me things about myself that only I knew, but she asked me if I wanted to try and work with the light. I said yes. We were sitting in her living room. I was on the couch and she was sitting in a chair about four feet in front of me. What happened next is still a mystery to me today. She started chanting the word Ohm, and she went into a kind of trance like state. My eyes started picking up subtle changes in light around her face and hair. The whole room glowed brighter with a golden light. Her eyes seemed to get darker and more piercing. A glow around her head and shoulders looked like a white aura about 5 inches off her outline. My eyes started to water and I felt a bit scared. After she stopped chanting Ohm, she sat quietly and asked me " what do you see?" I slowly told her what I saw. Her face seemed to almost disappear in the light while another face shined through. I saw a dark haired masculine man with a beard fade in and out. Similar to a hologram, when

Tide and the Crannog

I blinked, or tried to talk it would fade away, but if I sat quietly with my eyes wide open it would fade in and out with different levels of definition. This all went on for about 3 to 5 minutes, and then slowly all the gold light in the background and shadows on her face would cease completely, and I was left sitting in front of this woman of very unique abilities. I am not sure what to make of this experience. I have seen her 3 times over 15 years and all three times I had similar experiences. I guess these encounters did not move me as profoundly as they did my brother. Maybe I am missing something of great importance, or maybe I am not ready, or willing to know what those visions entail.

This book is part autobiographical, and part self help spiritual guide, sharing many of the personal lessons learned, and wisdom gained in the first 35 years of Ryan's life. It sometimes reads like a personal diary or journal giving you insight into the author's state of mind at the time. It is also filled with very valuable core values, or codes to live by, that were self discovered after being burned, injured, or victorious in life.

Finally it is a great honor to be asked by my brother to participate in this very personal creative project, and write this foreword. It is in his creative style and thoughtfulness that this collection of ideas and words has manifested. It was written in part to help others who may find these words enlightening; and in part to leave a family heirloom for those grandchildren and descendants not yet born into this world.

...Something unsettled in my body,
first came from pain and
struggled to survive,
then conquered an oppressor.
Then a girl stepped on my heart;
both of these have been healed;
a woman now truly loves me and
death I will face willingly.
Still the body is telling me
something is unsettled.....

Woe and Apophenia

There is in everyone (divine power) existing in latent condition. This is one power divided above and below; generating itself, making itself grow, seeking itself, finding itself, being mother of itself, father of itself, sister of itself, spouse of itself, daughter of itself, son of itself. Unity, being a source of the entire circle of existence. – Hyppolytus

According to Klaus Conrad **apophenia** is more or less the act of seeing patterns or connections in random and meaningless data. It is usually attributed to the over sensitivity of the brain in often times healthy individuals. So the act of one's daily life becoming or showing signs of synchronicity could be placed in this category. I also think the science of studying fractals falls in line as well. A fractal is the detection of a pattern, or form, in something thought to be fluid or formless. A good example is that of the foam from a breaking ocean wave. Could you imagine trying to connect the dots of a breaking wave into a reoccurring pattern? Fractals tend to be a smaller version of the thing in which they belong, so the micro cosmic version of a breaking wave is found in the macro cosmic wave itself. Each is unique to the present moment and is still connected by the same ordering to create a pattern.

Woe is the resentment or grief or regretful feeling that we all feel at times. Like when you find yourself questioning what you're going to do with your life. I often think that the woeful feeling is overcome by the act of apophenia in one's life. The feeling of a pattern and an order gives us meaning in our lives. On the other hand we know all too well the people who stretch their limited ideas into a metaphysical connection that just isn't there. These people are in line with the egocentric grasping of trying to fit in and feel important, I think we all do it sometimes. The terrible thing is when these desperate graspers try to sell it to you, how dishonest and low they become. Nonetheless, synchronous energy plays a powerful role in our awareness. It links us to our path in life, it is however, often difficult to detect accurately.

People in different locations often report having the same psychic or paranormal experiences; or they play a role in the same dream at the same time. These types of events are actually very common but are overlooked, or just hidden. How many times have you been thinking of someone intensely, and then a few minutes later the phone rings, and there they are? These types of things are acts of synchronicity. When my older brother was born, my grandmother made a phone call to the hospital in Montreal. When she reached my mother on the line, she said "it's a boy". This occurred without her knowing that my mother was even in labor, grandma just intuitively knew a newborn baby boy was here.

I often think that the major events in our lives are much more "apopheanic" than we know. The births, deaths, tragedies, breakups, accidents, sicknesses, jobs, vacations are all sort of small signs along the path of life to put us through the experiences we need to become more self aware. These signposts will ultimately teach us key points that we as individual souls need in order to become more evolved and enlightened. I once was in Ireland with my brother near the small town of Navan. We were visiting the family of our close friend Seamus. His father James McGeough drove us around at high RPM's in his three cylinder car. We were having a blast. These are some of the best friends, and best people I've ever met. We went to the round tower, and then to the river Boyne, and then to a place called Slain Castle. When we arrived the castle was closed and we parked just across the street because we couldn't drive in. The castle has a high stone gate at the front drive-in entrance; the gate is so large that you can't see over it, without climbing up a little to grab the iron bars and peek over. We pulled up and knew immediately it was closed, but as we walked toward the front gate I was sent to another place in my mind. I went to a dream state, like a déjà vu kind of feeling. I knew already what I was about to see. I had dreamt years before of the place I was now standing in. I didn't know it was a real place until this moment, but the dream I had was vivid, and like most of my dreams very lucid. So as I was walking, I paused and this dream came rushing back to me in all its fine details. I could sense the event unfolding just before it happened. I told myself about the vista that I was about to gaze upon just before I climbed up the stone wall gate. Sure enough I was right; I'd seen this castle before in my dream. There was only one thing missing, a small river or creek on the left side of the castle. I didn't see it, but in my dream it was apparent, it was surely there. I looked for a while and asked James if he thought there might be a creek down there. He pondered and mapped out the area in his head, then said, "Yes, it should flow through the property somewhere down there." I looked more intently, and then eventually could see in the distance a spot where the thick trees were hanging out over a small pool of water. My confirmation was here, the creek was there, just hidden by the dense growth of trees hanging, branched out over the creek. I knew at that moment that something synchronistic was happening. I felt I was in the exact place in the world, and in my life, that I was supposed to be. A small sense of peace and freedom followed me through the rest of my stay on the emerald isle.

> *The human eye is the mother of distance. It is a startling truth that how you see, and what you see, determine how, and who you will be.* – Jon O'Donahue

The point here is to never forget the mystery and wonder of the place where we live, and the life we live. It is so apparent when we stop, and just relax for a moment, and think of all the things we have witnessed; the routine things we do every day, the countries, and the people we encounter. The life we have is incredible. Sitting still I see a plant, or a bird, or the wind in the trees, and I am reminded of how wild this life is. I just get on a plane, and hours later I am across the world visiting another country where people live in a completely different way.

It is the mind that creates want and fulfills it. – Yogananda

There is some sort of synchronous pattern to all our lives, and I know that the more attuned we are to these little events, the more grounded we become, and the more our lives have meaning. We must be going somewhere or evolution wouldn't even exist. Since it does, and we see it all around us, in all species, we get the feeling that there is meaning and purpose driving us to evolve and become better. Yes, some progressive evolution is violent and cutthroat, but all of nature has both creative and destructive qualities. We are always becoming and always renewing, this is why we intuitively know each and every one of our lives has meaning. Never forget the wonder of the world.

It is where two come together that one exists – the razor's edge sharpens, sharpens bliss. None can create it nor can they destroy, but all can transfigure it, from it we are born. The razor's edge is sharp and still, it can always cut. It's will and yours are the same, open or shut. Catching the wind is the essence, and it is the dream; both are leading while following. Though we try to find the questions to all the answers we display, it would still be the same if said the other way. Liberate the heart and mind by living through the soul, we can make the slope a mountain, don't choose to make it a hole. The old man river is eternally flowing wet, even on the edges in which he beset. Though he rises to cool the air, go back to the riverbed, and he is always there.

The overall message in all of this is one of self discovery which is something we are constantly embarking on naturally. The difficult part of the process is that it is you yourself discovering you yourself; which means that the process is subjective. There is no way around it. You are all that you have to detect yourself. This entire book is predicated upon the idea that consciousness is the ground of being. The tool used to quantify consciousness is consciousness itself; so then again, it is a subjective process. It is not a product or process of the brain. It is the source of our reality, world, and experience. Many sciences are aiming to prove that consciousness is in fact a secretion of the brain; and if we gather enough information about brain function then we will understand consciousness. However, the fallacy with this approach is that it is still detected by a human being using their consciousness, which again is completely subjective. Many ancient teach-ings and philosophies maintain that the only way to understand consciousness is to understand thy self. Ancient sages have said that consciousness is the ground of being simply because it connects all of creation and all life. So to take it a step further, we do not create creation, but creation creates us; or we do not create consciousness, but consciousness create us. We learn of ourselves, by ourselves, which is why we all possess the power to will ourselves to a higher state of consciousness. The process of doing so is to love oneself; and the treasure of righteousness is love.

Two

Iris of the Child

Lying in bed and reading, I was paused in contemplation of the many meanings to do with the spiritual nature of human beings. As nature enters every scene and activity that we do I see the pattern of things found in nature. The thoughts about why tall trees make us feel connected and the scent of fresh pine needles trigger emotions and memories of myself as a natural and sentient being.

10

Tide and the Crannog

I reach out to the low hanging pine needles, pick some off and with sappy fingers bring them to my nose with the second nature of eating or breathing, something I did without thinking. These smells poised in my sinuses hit the **brau** and my eyes squint with the recollection of hundreds of thousands of years' familiarity.

I hunted as young boy in Georgia, my house was in the area said to be the highest point in my town, I could see no other house higher than mine with the exception of my next door neighbor's. I was among the last to be dropped off after school because the bus had to make the trek to the top of Manoleta Drive. Grabbing my pump bb-gun I am headed down the steep back yard walking under the porch poles, black metal and hollow, they make the sound of ringing wire when I hit them as I pass by. The sound travels up some thirty feet to the bottom of the wooden porch, gray with weathering treatment and carpenter bees flying all around the bottom wood. We would hit the bees with tennis rackets when we were up on top. My best pal Randolph was the kid who exposed me to hunting. I did it because I knew it made me tough and cool at school, but I did surely enjoy it.

I would even go alone, I enjoyed it enough to seek out small game; birds and squirrels, shoot them and retrieve them and bury them. To get to the burial ground you had to walk through three other yards full of exposed granite popping in and out of the bushy moist grass. Then at a clearing, and a flat yard that followed the pastures fence was a hundred yards of rolling granite. Marbled and gray and warm to walk on, I'd take my kills to the edge of the thick forest growing on both sides of the barbed wire fence. As I crawl under the brush, there is a sandy and moist spot in the trees where the pine needles, dead and brown make it easy to dig mini graves with small sticks. I'd dig little holes evenly spaced and put my little dead birds and squirrels in their shallow holes. Covering them up, feeling spooky and that somehow I've done a respectable thing, a noble thing, I'd scamper out

11

from under the brush and look at the cows and bulls in the pasture.

I remember looking at my little graves when I'd hunt and find no birds to shoot at in the trees, this happened a lot. I always thought I must be killing all the birds and I shouldn't hunt too often. Those graves were on the way to the best spot to climb the barbed wire fence. Through the trees the circular hay bales were smashed up against the fence and bulging through, and a foot higher. I'd climb the bales from my side and make it over without any real risk of getting stuck with a barb. You can walk on the bales and fall between them and get close to the cows without any chance of getting tested by a bull. The smells are wet and muddy and the seat of my pants was cold from sitting on hay too long. I felt adventurous. We were in the pasture, we knew we weren't supposed to be in there but we did it all the same anyway. When I was there with Randolph, we had a blast and so much fun, two kids with guns and hundreds of acres to survey. We'd just have fun trying to shoot the cows with bb's, mostly trying to hit the bulls' dick and get them to jump or something. When I was there alone it was different. Shaded by big trees and on the dangerous side of the fence I felt connected to the earth. I also felt a little scared, of what I didn't know. I think being alone with no one anywhere near me made me feel vulnerable. I'd ponder things and find myself lost in thought for long spells. I'd come up with questions that had no answers, like what would I look like when I am an adult of 30 years old. I don't know how much time I'd think about that but I know I'd try to envision my adult face and be boggled with a vision of no form.

Even better what would I look like when I was eighty, the only likeness I could get was pale skin and white hair, but no real features. My connection to nature was apparent from an early age; I'd feel unique and special when I arrived back at home, somehow peaceful. My little journeys were mostly spent by myself because Randolph lived about fif-

Tide and the Crannog

teen minutes away by car. We were great pals who trusted each other and shared the need to be tough, and act like men. When I visited him we strolled through his neighborhood called Bramble Wood. He had a good creek that got pretty deep in some places. Walking straight through, soaking my shoes and pants we'd find fool's gold and crawdads, and once we found a small snake. I lifted a log in the creek and the little snake slithered under an adjacent log but its striped tail hung out in broad daylight wavering in the stream. I just reached in with lightning speed and grabbed it, took two steps toward the bank of Georgia red clay and threw it on land next to him. We both poked at it and got a good look before we lost it again in the creek. Moments like these create puddles of memory in the back of my childhood mind.

We always cared for each other and honor and respect were a part of our friendship, even at twelve years old. We always backed one another up in fights at school or if we got in trouble with the teacher. I remember the feeling of a real friend at such a young age, I'm sure it has imprinted me to find good people throughout my adult life, but as time splashes us daily and relentlessly, I do lose that feeling. The genuine character of people seems hidden behind the day to day survival of wealth and status. I do see the genuine friendship still but I myself am chasing the same dragons of the better tomorrow and I find clouds in my mind because of it. I know, regardless of what I have today, I can have none of it when I die.

Randolph and I would sometimes walk for miles to get to some place for some reason. It was always someplace new, and to us somehow dangerous. We walked through the woods on the other side of the creek just to get to the main road in a roundabout way, just to know we did it. There was a cleared small path where large cement manholes were laced through the thick woods. I don't remember for sure but there was no path or road to get the heavy bulldozers and heavy equipment back there to build

13

those manhole things. They were spaced about every one hundred yards and were as tall as we were. They were about four feet high and maybe six feet across. When we reached the road, cars were cruising by now and then, but the woods were so thick we stood fifteen or twenty feet in the bush and no car, even if slow moving, could see us. So we did what any adventure seeker would do. We threw rocks at fast moving cars and ducked down as they went by, and yes we hit them.

Probably the worst thing we did in his neighborhood was in the field just across the street from his house. On his side were houses but across the street was just a meadow, then woods, then the creek. We were in the meadow and the grass was up to our waist and chest, so we, I mean I, took a lighter and lit a little blade of grass on fire. He looked at me and I looked back, waited a few seconds and watched the flames grow to about the size of a basketball. I then began to stomp the flames out and as I stomped more grass went up, he watched and at some point he started to stomp also. It was probably only two minutes or so when we were done but I looked at him and he looked at me and we were in a full sweat and adrenalized to the hilt. Around us was a twenty or thirty foot black and charred burnt circle. We got the hell out of there and knew we were lucky we didn't watch any longer. This event I knew was entirely my fault, and I owned up to it. It just caught on fire so fast, it was moving as fast as we were. I might never forget that day. We never told anyone and I guess we were far enough off the road to where no one saw smoke and no one could see the charred circle. I always looked for it when I was on the road but never told anyone. I could just imagine burning down those woods and the neighboring houses.

We were competitive and did well at anything we attempted as a team but through adolescence Randolph grew bigger and stronger than I. We shared grade-school girlfriends and both entered art contests. At some point He moved out of that house and across town to where I had never been.

Tide and the Crannog

I remember sneaking out at night in my neighborhood, usually to do something destructive. But sometimes we just set out to be out there in that dark world while everyone else was sleeping. It was exciting and exhausting at the same time. We were kids, so we walked everywhere and sometimes many miles. When we returned we were easily asleep in minutes. One night we called a girl, Jenny from the neighborhood through the woods. She and we always promoted kissing and playing games that tested our level of sexuality, needless to say I enjoyed it, and I think we all did. This night we talked on the phone and made plans to meet halfway between our neighborhoods, in the woods by a small pond. It was set for 1am, at the Cameron pond. The moon was full and lit up everything, this was a big help because the Cameron pond was no doubt spooky, and a night without a moon was out of the question for such a meeting place.

Jenny had met us there before. We just walked and talked about the houses we'd look at and who the people inside were. We'd flirt and kiss and play games. This night she didn't show up and we were perturbed, very perturbed. After all we walked a long way for nothing. We then decided to head toward her house. Maybe she would be coming down the hill toward us. No, she never showed. After walking a while we were almost to her house and we decided to go the distance, and go all the way to her house. She lived with her mother and two sisters. All of the lights were out and her home in slumber. We cased the property and threw sticks and stuff at her window. We gave it a serious try and she never came to the window. We went all that way for nothing, not even a little kiss. Randolph and I were now really upset and dreading the walk home. We ransacked our thoughts, as well as Jenny's garage. Soon enough we had her bicycle and thought at least we'd get some transportation home. We didn't think twice as we both held on to the bike down the long hill to the road adjoining our domains. One sat on the seat while the other stood on the pedals. It was not a ride made for comfort but hell; it cut our time in half.

Half was down hill, then the other half was all up hill; once to the flats we walked the bike all the way to the top of my neighborhood. There was some discussion about what to do with the bloody bike. We couldn't keep it, so we looked back down the last little hill from the top of my neighborhood. There was a small hill with an equally sized hill opposing it, it was a perfect gully. We always called it the top of Chaparral. With good spirit and feeling totally justified we ghost rode the bike down the hill knowing it would wither to its final destination in the middle somewhere. We heaved the two-wheeler down the hill and smiled as it glided to the bottom with no rider, and made it a little ways up the other side, then bounced over the curb into the outskirts of a neighbor's yard. It was a wee bit bent and damaged, then we walked the short distance home.

At school we were no doubt accused by Jenny for the dirty deed, but we denied it with a grin. "You should have met us like you said instead of standing us up. You could have ridden your bike to meet us, but now that is not an option". She was very frustrated with us but as time went on and days went by, I saw that bike sitting in the corner of a yard. I recall it must have laid there lifeless for weeks before it disappeared. These are the juvenile things we did as kids, we called it fun.

In high school we were still strong friends and I'd introduce him to my pals and vice versa, it was fun to have friends in other school districts. I'm pretty sure he was better off than I was. At sixteen he had a car and I could borrow my mom's. I remember not being able to do some things that he and his friends could do, like go skiing for the weekend, but he did take me duck hunting in South Carolina for the first time. I was smaller than him, but as tough as I could be with my foul mouth and arrogant attitude. When I was challenged, I'd tell my opponent how I was going to destroy him in front of anyone who was there; it worked up until I was about seventeen. I always knew before I entangled myself in a losing battle to leave or not get involved because I was dealing with much stronger kids in high school. Some of which had broken facial bones and bloody noses. My school was rough. There were times when I'd choose to prove myself, and when I chose to, I always did. I managed to win once my line was crossed and all my anger came to the surface.

The worst thing about spending time with Randolph was being forced to attend church with his family. Even at twelve I could sense the phony grin of those with open mouths and open hands asking for money; and I did pay attention, something about them was just not right. The churches in rural and suburban Georgia just do whatever the hell they want with the flock. I've been to many of them as a child and participated in singing and Boy Scout retreats all designed to infiltrate the mind of the youth with the distraction of something fun. It's not unlike when parents appease their kids with distracting candy to get them to conform; it works on most of them. Even the kids singing songs to Jesus because they loved him, sounded soul-less and contrived, these attitudes are groomed and subverted by a pastor or a parent hiding their guilt.

When Randolph and I became young adults we visited each other less and less. I moved to the west coast for college and to be near the ocean. I've always had an affinity for the ocean. Sometimes so much I feel stuck being so close to it, I won't move away. Many good opportunities have come my way just as I watch them drift by because they would have taken me to drier land or city life somewhere else. He said he would come visit me when I left but a few years went by and phone calls weren't returned, I was puzzled. Life was taking us in our own unique directions. I could see that something was different. One day, on the phone, his churches' voice came out of him as he tried to save my soul. I was shocked he felt the need to cleanse me so, after all he knew me from when we were just little adventurers, he knew who I was, and he knew what kind of person I was. The conversation was long and going really to no resolve. I told him my soul didn't need saving because it was eternal, and had no purpose tucked away saved and awaiting a rainy day. These were words I'd borrowed from my exposure to the California culture of eastern philosophy and liberal mindedness. Through frustration he damned me to hell unless I would accept Jesus into my heart, since that was the only way to reach the kingdom of heaven. I responded with heaven being a place here and now in the heart and mind, and that I didn't have to wait or save myself to get there. So now I was told to fear the wrath of God or be cast out. And I talked about God being a loving entity that would never want to instill fear and doubt into his children. The fear would be counterproductive to the evolution of a spiritual being on their way to expanding consciousness. Fear would only fragment me and make it harder to open up into something whole. Ultimately we argued and the phone call ended with each of us on our own side, sadly we haven't spoken since. Thirteen years of friendship gone, cast out to the land of Nod.

When we were kids we watched a civil war movie on television where two soldiers on opposing sides of the war had to reluctantly battle each other, only they had grown up as best friends as kids. Neither of them wanted to fight, so they avoided killing one another. When the battle was over one ripped a dollar bill in half and gave half to the other, and they went their separate ways. One day when the war was over they met and put that bill back together. I've always thought that someday something like this might happen to me, us. Randolph and I may meet again as pals.

Three

Witches and Queens

The heart is a well-spring of energy and power. We all know what it's like to feel great and on top of the world but yes we all know what it's like to be down and broken hearted. When I was in high school I chased this girl with yellow blonde hair and eventually caught her. I had to coerce her into dating me which was something I usually didn't have to do. She was amazingly beautiful to me; petite and curvy even for a young woman, still fit and athletic. She seemed a little dumb but I didn't care at all, I had to have her. I had her in my bedroom and was flirting and touching her and making her as comfortable as possible. I had been trying for weeks to get her to take her clothes off and one night she did. From that day on I was in love. She had a body suit under her jeans that snapped or better yet unsnapped at her crotch. She showed me what was down there and when she did she knew she had me right where she wanted me. I succumbed to her beautiful body and fantastic curves; I was hers to do with whatever she wanted. A few months later, after professing our love to each other I was told by one of my close friends that she showed him and another guy her pretty parts as well. Although she wasn't having sex with either of them and she was with me, I was shocked and in disbelief. These two guys were very good friends of mine so I was inclined to trust them.

They were telling the truth, after confronting her I could read her face when she lied to me. After a few minutes she confessed and said she could do whatever she wanted. I was crushed, and as time passed I became desperate to keep her and tell her about my love for her, but it only pushed her further away. Those same friends reported to me that her car was at another guys house as they drove passed on the way home from school. I was at soccer practice every day so I would have no way to know. This happened many times and finally I had to see for myself. My friend Macarowitz and I drove by one afternoon, and sure enough, her car was at one of the football player's houses, in the middle of the driveway. I knew then she was unfaithful, and I confronted her once again. This time she didn't deny it, she admitted it freely and stated that once again she can do whatever she wants. She had been having sex with the two of us all along, even as she professed her love for me.

I just couldn't take it, so I verbally barraged her with shitty insults and watched as tears came flying out of her eyes. I actually enjoyed it; I cursed and told her exactly what she was. Then I cut off all communication, it was just the natural thing to do. She came back to me and professed her love again and we made love again, but I could never trust her again, and so it goes my first heartbreak.

My second heartbreak occurred as an adult. We lived together for a couple of years and made a home warm and cozy. But this home was not allowed to have my creative thought or influence placed upon it; it was all hers, the house was hers! The selfish side of a witchy woman is often very deeply subverted and if you give them your heart you will never see it again until it's too late. All she ever talked about was marriage and babies, even on our first date. I almost didn't call her after the first date for that reason alone. I told her I didn't want marriage any time soon, she said no problem she could wait. At first I was dating multiple women and loving it, I had developed a streak over the past year or so, seeing about one girl each month.

This woman, who really turned out to be a girl, was different. She had a drive for me and it turned me on. It also turned out to be short-lived and then turned me off. Her maternal instinct was keeping me around and ultimately destroyed a genuine good love. I admit I really liked the attention and care she gave me, but it was only an act, an elaborate act. She held up her act for two years and was pretty convincing, however when someone has ulterior motives and you live with them, they most certainly surface over time. She couldn't stand it anymore, knowing the man she lived with was not going to become the dream she had been dreaming for years. I was not going to give her a baby, that job was to be filled by the next guy whose application was approved based on debt to income ratio, naivety and gullibility.

The little box that has an American dream package inside won't fit around me. I won't fit in that little box; I just can't if I am to be true to myself as a human being. I was bending as much as possible without selling my heart and soul, it just didn't work. I learned a lot from that time in my life, mostly that all people are selfish to some degree. Many people are so selfish they have no self to be aware of, only material ideas and things to possess. You can't possess another person, people are a gift that they choose to give to you, or they choose not to. Love/relationships don't fit into boxes, they don't keep up with the neighbors, and they don't have anything to do with money.

I think the fear of not having a perfectly controlled relationship has destroyed the one we had. The fear of becoming her mother became apparent as well. She was so afraid of making the wrong choices in marriage; she attracted exactly what she was afraid of. I also think it is likely to happen over and over again, her fear of being alone and without money and without a baby, will drive many away and dampen those that try to stay. All of this came to light for me when I realized that she didn't love me. I was lying in a hospital bed; it was the first time I had been hospitalized since I was born.

We had just arrived home from Bali, Indonesia, driven two hours from LAX airport after a twenty hour flight. Needless to say we were tired and the bed was as nice as anticipated. When I awoke I didn't feel so good but attributed it to jet lag and body clock malaise. Off to work I went and immediately noticed a bad headache, as usual I just ignored it. At work I also noticed a lack of energy and some dizziness, I told the restaurant manager about it, as well as the highlights of the trip. Pushing on, I soon realized I was going to have to deal with this throughout the day; I barely made it through my shift and headed home. I called in sick for the following day, then took ibuprofen and ate and relaxed. When she arrived home I spilled my complaints and was brushed off with toughen up talk and get over it sentiment, this was the normal attitude from her when pain was the issue. The next morning hoping for relief, I was disappointed by more and worsening body aches, and a severe headache. I went through a few hours and knew this was serious, I had never felt this bad in my life. So I went to a local community clinic that treated the less fortunate who can't afford health care. They drew my blood and sent it to the lab, I waited thinking the next day surely I'd feel better.

Two days passed and in the morning the call came in. Is this Ryan? Yes it is. You need to get to the emergency room right away, you have tested positive for gram negative bacteria in your blood, and this is very serious. She was there and heard the conversation. She drove me to the hospital and I told the clerk what I had. They rushed me straight in with no waiting; lots of ill people were looking at me with disdain, as I got the privilege to cut in line. I was poked and prodded, blood drawn again and tested. I remember asking them what is **bacteremia** and how long I would be in the hospital? The nurses said, you will be here until we find out exactly what you've got. I replied, will I be here over night, he said yes. I said more than one night, he said yes, until we cure you. The fear set in.

This sucked, relinquishing control to strangers with needles. They narrowed it down to a few likely diseases; malaria, dengue fever, yellow fever, typhoid fever, shingles, or hepatitis. Two days of tests and they diagnosed me with salmonella typhoid, typhoid fever. Let me just say this fucking sucks. I had three doctors who had never treated it, and who apparently didn't speak to each other. I asked so many questions and mostly received "we just don't know" answers.

As this all went down, she was the one calling my parents, brothers, and friends to inform them. I could see the disdain and lack of want in her face when my mom called for updates. She couldn't hide it, she stayed in the hospital with me, but she no longer cared. I listened to her complain about dealing with the phone calls, and saying the same thing over and over to different people. I couldn't believe that she was complaining about informing my family of my condition while I was splayed out with a deadly disease. She was sitting there but with no tenderness, no empathy, no connection in her eyes. She talked about herself a lot, and the things she wanted, her goals in life. She asked me how I was going to pay for the hospitalization, as well as my bills, and rent. After all, I had only worked one day in the last month. I didn't know how I would manage to pay; I had a social worker who was on my side, (thank God for social workers) that's all I really knew.

One day she brought me food and sat with me in my hospital room. I complained about the old man sharing the room with dementia. He stood up about every half hour and walked out of the room attached to all those machines. He did this all night long. He was calling for his wife who wasn't there. Each time the cords would pull out of the machines they would beep loud as hell signaling the nurses. The nurses rushed in and put him back to bed. This went on all night so I slept very little,

We ate and as she left, I waddled over to the window where I could watch her walk across the parking lot to her car. She headed down the stairs and pulled out her cell phone and was talking to someone. I watched her intently and missed the looks she used to give me when she believed in me. She buzzed across the parking lot, never seeing me watching her. I knew then that she didn't love me anymore.

Home a few days from the hospital, I was feeling terrible and still on an intravenous antibiotic drip for another ten days. She gave more of the coldness and less sympathy. I knew we were headed for the rocks but didn't want to deal with it due to the stresses of my condition; it came to the surface anyway. We talked about going our separate ways and how the details would be worked out. I was surprised and couldn't believe she could do this at such a critical time, but she did just like that, lickity-split. We made plans for me to move out of the house but with time to heal, get off the I.V., and get back to work. We slept in separate beds and didn't talk; I was hurting inside and slowly growing resentful. A few days of the awkward lifestyle and she had had enough; she couldn't take it anymore. So she kicked me out and demanded I leave as soon as possible. As far as I could tell, she wanted me gone so she could pursue another man, it was a hunch but turned out to be correct.

A little luck came my way by the first phone call I made to rent another property. I landed a stellar studio apartment on a beautiful horse property; it was actually a friend of hers which she gave me her blessing on. She just wanted me out, and any way she could do it was fine with her. Just like that, I moved with no money, out of work, and sicker than I've ever been in my life. The life of being a zombie and being exhausted from it had just begun. I had no choice but to move on, to heal, In fact I was so focused on healing myself I didn't realize that my emotional state and my heart were in a quagmire of stench. I lay in bed and wondered how a woman who professed her love for me daily could do such a thing. How can someone beg you to move in together, start a home, pick out curtains, ask you to make babies, ask you to marry them, and sleep with you every night, then suddenly say " I don't love you anymore, love is not enough"? I always thought that love was enough, it was exactly that! Love was what ultimately mattered between people; love is what being in a relationship was all about. I told her I loved her and I didn't want to leave in such a petty way. She said: "It didn't matter and that love was not enough". I said love is enough and without it we have nothing. I lay in bed and realized she and I had nothing.

I called her father just before I left the house we shared, for his advice, he and I had always seemed to get along. He told me he thought of me as a son and that he hoped we would stay together and get through this, it gave me some hope. The chips fell in their places and I came to find she had placed her hope in another suitor, she was laying her legs upon an other's bed. I moved out, we didn't speak again.

Love can be suicide, it happens when you feel blessed enough to open yourself up enough to share.

Tide and the Crannog

As we all try to genuinely share, the things we share are spiritual fragments. You trust another to hold and care for your fragment/shards. Mine, I decided to give to her, over time she tucked them away faster and faster, then she craved more. I knew I was committing suicide but figured I was man enough to handle what may come. Now and then she stabbed me with a chard; I figured this was the sacrifice one makes for lasting love. I thought someday she'll grow and overcome her selfishness. I was trying to be a mirror, reflecting and un-judging. Instead I shattered with my own fragments thrust into me. She joyfully picked the time of a great struggle to begin battle. Then I knew it was forever, I knew I was the only one committed to the suicide. Her fear had stopped her from committing to hers. She gave me her shards as well, and staring at them reminds me how sharp they were when she first gave them to me. I am a man but still handled them gently, and in good faith, for I knew someday she would need them back. We all need them at times. I won't be able to watch over them, care and clean them any longer. She will need them someday and my only course is to leave them here in the earth, under a willow tree. She doesn't even remember giving them to me.

My healing is body and emotion and spirit too. I have no choice. I must carefully fit my broken shards into their proper places. It is so rare to see them whole. My throat stuck with tears from shock and disbelief will need to heal and sing again. Life and love can cause so much pain, and we suffer through this world and the next, always trying to love. We are always trying to commit suicide and I once again remember why, because in dying and loving we realize it never ends! My head rings with frustration but I am given a lesson, one that inspires me to make it one of my own, and keep it in my life. I decided before this to develop a code of ethics, a basic code for better living. This is one of nine lessons I will keep; *Always get back on your horse.* Yes it's very simple, but none the less pertinent.

**Always get back on your horse,
there is no time or place for self pity,
it gets you nowhere.**

There are some queens in the world as well, I am most fortunate to have shared love and time with a few, or maybe just two. The women who are queens are rare and unique in the quality of being unselfish. Even as all people are selfish, a few are selfish only for their own survival. These women are grounded in caring and loving. The biggest part of who they are is ruled by their heart, not their emotion. When you get to know a queen, the first thing you learn is that they are not materialistic at all. They know they have all they need inside themselves, and they find lucky men to teach this to, very lucky men. When a man, at any age, is shown the secret power of the queen, he is changed for the rest of his life. His heart is altered, and altered until his death. It's a kind of opening up, a kind of remembering your humanness. No matter how cloudy and frustrated with life a man gets, once touched by a queen, he is forever haunted by what it feels like to be loved.

Starting again when I was a child, about the same time I met Randolph, I saw the most beautiful girl I had ever seen, keep in mind I was twelve. She got on the bus at one of the last stops before we arrived at school. My house was among the first stops so I was at the back of the bus but I could see her beauty from back there. When we arrived at school we gathered in the lunchroom before we went to class. We were assigned seats and tables and she was directly across from me. I immediately started teasing her and poking fun at her, even though she was nice to me, I had no skillful way to show her how lovely she was. Her name was Amy and she had these naturally raised eyebrows that set her apart from any other girl in the entire school. Along with that her eyes were light and bright, and her childish skin rosy and tender in all the supple places so as to give her a glow.

Somehow over the next week or so I convinced her that I liked her and we began our little courtship. I eventually got my mom to drive me to her house one afternoon, it had been raining and she dropped me on the long gravel driveway lined with woods of pine trees. I remember being excited to see her. I had on what I thought was my best sweater and the heavy wet drops landed on both sides of the driveway. The heavy pine branches let go of dewy drops that slap the ground as I walk. It was not raining at the time but a rhythm of delicate drops landed all around me. As I approached the house three dogs ran my way barking, they stopped me in my tracks. I stood there for what must have been ten minutes scared and talking to each dog, they just looked me in the eye and growled and barked, nobody came out of the house. I had candy I brought for her but reluctantly gave it to the canines to appease them. As I did, a van came down the driveway and stopped and asked me if I needed help. I stated my business, the woman driver was dropping off a friend for Amy's brother, and I made it safely inside. I'll never forget that day, when I received my first taste of love from a girl, from a queen.

I would later become a jerk and cause us to break up a couple of times. And as we grew into young adults we grew apart, dated other people and I moved away. In college I moved to California, met one other queen and many more witches and made friends too. It would be seventeen years later before Amy and I spoke to each other again. I had always felt fond of her and the way she was sweet-hearted. Over the years I thought about her, always wanted to meet a woman like her. One day after thinking about her for months, I decided to try to contact her. It was easier than I thought, a little time on the Internet and I had an address and phone number, it turned out to be her uncle, he was as nice as nice could be, full of southern hospitality; gave me her number. I called and she answered, and the flood of memories made puddles in the back of my brain, it was a surreal experience. She was as sweet as the last time I had seen/spoke to her, I couldn't believe it. I told her my reasons for contacting her as odd as they may be. Basically I told her I never forgot the time we shared as children, even as young kids I remember the feelings I had with her. I told her she was the first girl I ever loved. We connected and wrote to one another over the next couple of weeks, bringing past experiences of my life to the forefront of my mind. "You see I believe that my time with you was my first taste of love with a girl. Please don't laugh; I am not looking for confirmation from you, that's not what this is about. It's really about me and what I want in my life. It's a process of recapitulation of meaningful and heartfelt events I am bringing to the surface, it's a spiritual endeavor. The recapitulation frees up energy that may be stagnant and getting drawn into less important things. My life has been rough lately but is fine at the moment. I got typhoid fever while surfing in Indonesia in June. The disease almost killed me, and so I've been doing a lot of reflecting and reassessing of what is important to me. I'm fine now and back to working and surfing. Contacting you is something I knew I had to do even before I got sick."

She sent me photos of her family and children; she was married for the second time. She gave me a brief synopsis of her life. "My life has been pretty crazy, I was actually searching for you about a week ago on the computer and think I found your brother, not sure though. You must have felt the vibe. I moved to Charleston in 1994, got married when I was 20 and divorced by the time I was 22, so that was fun, (hint of sarcasm). After that I just partied all the time, now that was really fun. I knew if I kept going like that I'd kill myself. I met my current husband and straightened myself out and in 2000 had my first child, then my second in 2003. I never did the soul searching thing I was too scared."

29

Tide and the Crannog

I replied "this is mind blowing huh; I am so glad you received my call and were so open to talking. I must have been picking up your vibe and choose now to make contact, but in all honesty I've wanted to contact you for years now. I was fortunate enough to realize that my contacting you was inevitable for me. I believe in my mind the connections we make as children can be a strong source of who we become as adults. The soul searching is a never ending saga and we only get closer if we try, so I try, especially when times are hard. I am trying to stay in the present moment and truly live and enjoy it. I do know for sure I am an expansion of consciousness and the untapped possibilities are immense."

We talked more and more and she blew my mind. She told me on the phone that she kept a note that I had written when I was about twelve that asked her to "go with me", in my town, this meant will you be my girlfriend. I wrote the note and attached it to flowers. I was absolutely amazed when she scanned it and e-mailed it to me and I could see my own hand writing. She must have had some reason to keep it all these years. She wrote back "I am truly honored and touched by everything you said in your e-mail. Truly, wow, what an amazing man you have become, and my gosh, you look just as you always have in my mind, except I can't see the little freckles across your nose. We may have been kids, but children have very real and very valid feelings, I totally agree with that. I share your belief that there are important moments in our lives that shape the kind of people we become. I have several defining moments that happen even between the ages of two and three that I remember like they happened last week". She was my first queen, I will always have her in my heart just as that, there are others but not as pure as the first.

Between the rare occasions of spending quality time with a queen, for me there were many good girls of all perspective and stature, and as I said before a few witches. The second and probably the last queen in my life served such a unique role it is so hard to describe. Her name is Michelle and she was twenty one years older than I. We met at a restaurant that we both worked at; she was my new boss, and the general manager. I was instantly attracted to her and liked her personality. She was always downing herself in a sarcastic tone, always belittling herself. She was blonde and petite, and the only thing I didn't like was her cigarettes. We passed one another at work I would always flirt with her jokingly, but she always returned the gesture. I had asked her out on dates a couple of times but I always got the feelings she thought it was a joke, after all she was my boss.

I knew she liked red wine so one day I asked her to go get a bottle with me, she said fine and left it at that. I looked her in the eye and said when can we do this? She said nonchalantly whenever you want. I said tonight after work, I also said I am serious! She could see that this was no joke, and she said fine, and I demanded her phone number. I arrived at her apartment, with a bottle of decent merlot, might have been Clos Du Bois, we drank and talked and began to glow. It was fun and the lights in her place were dim. We talked about the world, places, culture, and romance. At some point I knew I was going to have to try to kiss her. It would have to wait for another night. I was nervous and didn't know if she was even interested in a nineteen year old man. Work was fine. We kept to ourselves and no one knew. It was a little secret.

After a couple of wine nights with the lights low and candles lit, I leaned in and went for the kiss. Within seconds we were intensely into one another's mouth, tongues cross teeth, and getting hotter. I didn't know what to do except keep going. It wasn't long before we were touching and I was amazed this mature woman was so passionate and letting me do the things I was doing. I loved it. We stopped for a moment then told each other to keep going, we did. Into the bedroom and the nudity was warm and sensual and exiting. We made love and I was on top of the world, it was good, and we fit together as if we had known each other before. We became a couple and did the things that couples do; only we didn't do them at work. No one at work ever knew. We both wondered when someone would see us out somewhere at night, for nine months no one did.

She had a son; he was just two years younger than I. I couldn't believe it. He was quiet and well mannered, and did what his mother told him. The two of them had a close bond. I could sense it when they were around each other. He was bigger than I, and in all honesty I thought for sure there would come a time when he'd challenge me for dating his mother. He never did. She commanded his respect, and she assured me that he understood; she told him that she and I had something real and special, so he respected her. He and I actually became friends and would talk when I was there at their home, it was so surreal. I'll never forget waking up in the morning and eating breakfast with the two of them, it was just normal. I'll always respect him for trusting his mother; I don't know if I could have done what he did, if I were in his shoes. I'll also never forget that one special amazing night in Point Loma. She and I bought a bottle of red wine, drove down to the end of the road at sunset cliffs and parked and walked around in the cool moonlit night. I took her down the eighty eight stairs leading to the bottom of cliff face; they were wet with sea mist and the plants dripping with the cold. She was nervous but excited; I could see her light up, that award winning smile, really more of a smirk.

We made it down and I knew the tide was low, so I grabbed her hand and hobbled over the uneven boulders, pools of puddles all around our feet. We went just about forty feet out toward the sea where a refrigerator sized rock cropped up. It was as wide as it was tall; we climbed on top of its wet flat surface. The two of us sat facing each other, uncorked the vino, and also some Parmesan cheese, it was perfect. We sat for longer than I anticipated, finished the bottle and gazed at each other in the full moon. I could see her perfectly, it was so bright, she was glowing, we were chilly and I kissed all over her. She was so happy, and seeing her smile so much made me happy. We worked our thighs to get up those stairs, got in the car and immediately got pulled over by the police. The cop asked us for identification and what were we doing there. Just looking at the ocean I said. She and I looked at each other and knew the officer thought she was my mother, he was cordial and he said "Have a nice night", and we laughed before we made it home and then made love.

We both knew what we had was quite unique and very real, but we both knew it would not last, neither of us was going to bring the other home to mother's for Thanksgiving dinner. We lasted in kind of sweet euphoria for nine months before I caused the break up. I sought out another woman who I knew before. I was intimate with her and then told Michelle about it, I knew this was a sure way to end it, it was childish and shallow. I knew for me it was time, I was never going to be able to go any further with her so I abruptly ended it. She knew what and why I had done it, and she accepted it, but surprised me when she took it harder than I expected. I think I was preparing myself all along, and she was not.

Before it ended, something magical happened, something so very difficult to explain. One morning after breakfast at her apartment, I was in the bathroom and on the mirror was a sticky note, a little two inch by two inch, yellow piece of paper. The note read "Antoinette" and included a phone number. I knew who this was but had never met her. She is the woman who my Michelle was often talking about. She was a clairvoyant and she was helping Michelle with spiritual endeavors. Michelle would have a session with this woman and come home and tell me all kinds of unreasonable things. Many things I was told were about me. I didn't believe a word, some woman I never met was talking about me and my relationship with my girlfriend and none sounded even remotely accurate. I told Michelle in the past that she was getting swindled and wasting

33

her money, but she swore the woman was truly gifted. I was sitting in the bathroom looking at this sticky piece of paper and I decided I was sick of this clairvoyant filling my girls head with lies. So I secretly wrote down the number and called and made an appointment. Little did I know two months later, when I met Antoinette for the first time, my life would be changed forever. My queen did a lot of wonderful things for me, but nothing ever given to me was as precious as my indirect introduction to Antoinette. I will thank her for the rest of my life, and she will always be my queen, and I love and respect her as such.

Four

THE LIGHT

The day for my meeting with Antoinette had arrived, just a normal day; I had to work that night but had half a day to do as I wish. I had spoken to her only once for directions to her home; the only thing she knew about me was my first name. I arrived in front of her house, parked the car and knocked on the door. She spoke to me from the side window, "just about five minutes and I'll be ready for you". Her voice was very soft and slow. I sat on one of the chairs in the tiny little yard. I was determined to give this woman a piece of my mind and tell her I could see through her vague readings of my Michelle.

The door opened and a person walked out and smiled briefly and walked by to their car and drove away. Meanwhile I looked at the woman standing in the door with a big smile. She looked nothing like the image I created in my mind, I was surprised. We went inside, introduced ourselves and sat. She was unlike any human I had ever seen. She had a thin neck and sort of wavy hair cut around her head. Her hands were obviously deformed and her fingers looked paralyzed and gnarled and shortened. She was a thinly built woman with a little roundness in the middle. Some other features about her structure were noticeably different; however I sensed a genuine happiness in her beautiful smile. Her eyes were blue.

She explained her gift to me and gave the history about her disease. She asked for an article of mine, anything that I wore will help her attune to my vibration. She needed the article to tap into her gift as it relates to me, I took off my necklace and handed it to her. She started a tape recorder to record the session and then she held her hands out to the air, closed her eyes and began to pray:

Heavenly Father, Divine Mother, all the great masters, by the word and the power of Paramahansa Yogananda, Jesus Christ, Mohavatar Babaji, Swami Sriyukteswar, Lihiri Mahashi, and saints and sages everywhere, to all the great masters, build a wall of living flame round about us and bless us in our quest for clarification, illumination , and healing. Aum....Peace....Amen.

I just watched and stared at her but prayed along also. I had never heard any of those names except for Christ and I decided years before that he wasn't responding to me.

As I watched her I immediately noticed a hue around her head and neck, a soft light almost white but blue hue. I remember it because it was the first time in my life I had ever seen anything like it. I shrugged it off as nothing. She finished the prayer and asked me what was the purpose in my visit and did I have any major concerns. I snidely replied I am here because of my girlfriend. She is one of your clients and I am here to prove to her that she is misguided by you. She seemed un-offended and asked simple questions like who is your girlfriend. All my replies were aloof and unhelpful. I didn't reveal Michelle's name to her. I knew she knew nothing about me and she has said many things about me to my girlfriend. I wanted to see if her powers could detect who I was and prove whether or not she was real. I offered her nothing in the way of who I was, all she had to go on was my first name and my necklace. She stopped talking about Michelle and started talking about me. She came up with names and genders and ages of people in my life. The conversation that ensued eventually left me dumbfounded. What took place that day made a lasting mark on my life…… forever. She said that I did not come to her by chance and that my intuition would reveal this in time.

She began to talk. She talked for about an hour and a half. I spoke less than twenty words the entire time and of these words I spoke mostly yes and no. She spoke of things no one could know, she talked about intimate strengths and fears I have. She told me about my perception of God and nature, about my relationships with family members, and friends. She even told me I was involved with a woman who is significantly older than me. She told me of my athletic career and problem areas in my body. Odd as it was, I had seen ten to twelve different doctors in the previous six months for a chronic foot injury that manifested into a chronic back injury. My healing began the moment I met her and over time I came back to see her for guidance concerning my injuries and this led to the opening of my spiritual side. These injuries took about six years of therapy to control and I am still in some subtle ways afflicted with them today, however I use my body daily for athletic activities. She gave me many treatment methods which I followed rigorously and I have no doubt that they were instrumental in my healing.

I was nineteen and somewhat naive but I knew from that day that Antoinette has true psychic powers. The solidification of such things is very personal and difficult to relay to others. I find that many people just don't understand or believe in things beyond their own five basic senses, which to me is just ridiculous. To the scientific community it is preposterous, none of us can see a subatomic particle with our limited human sense of sight, but still we know factually that they are here all around us, constantly. My solidification occurred not by the things she spoke but indubitably by the paranormal expanse I witnessed on that first day. I also experience similar touches of the spirit realm every time I see her and often times when I am alone. The light of a spiritual realm revealed to me; a shift in perceptual reality I can never un-know. The visual is so beyond description, it leaves a welt of opening in my psychic consciousness that I cannot forget.

We talked about higher states of consciousness and awareness, these things I had always been interested in, but I was jaded by a southern upbringing in the heart of the Bible belt. I grew up in a violent and hypocritical place; the Klu Klux Klan was out many weekends in full garb passing out literature and I went to school with their children. Thank God my parents were hippies, they taught me and my brothers to see the equality in people as well as in nature. I knew in school that I didn't always fit in, but I was saved and respected by my athletic pursuits.

On the first day of that first session with her, I had hope in my heart instead of grief and depression. I didn't show her the pain I was in but still she knew somehow. She shifted my perceptual awareness to a new and higher state. She told me details about my injury that were unknown to anyone at that time even me, it was astounding. She knew more about them than any doctor I had been diagnosed by. My injuries were so severe; I was terrified to acknowledge them. I remember a month or so before I met her I had a new sensation, it was when I realized I was depressed for the first time in my life. I was stretching in my living room, trying to stretch out the pain, but I was only making it worse. It was so bad I couldn't bend over to tie my shoes, it hurt to move my arms, it hurt to brush my teeth. I lay on the floor and felt agony flood over me, I was holding back tears. The frustration of a once strong athletic body turned to a bundle of chronic pain was finally too much for my mind to handle. I was so downtrodden I knew I could let myself die. Strangely I lay in the puddle of realization that I could consciously leave this body behind and face the process of death. In my core I was shocked, I can only explain the knowing of my own power to let go of this physical body. I laid there in my quagmire of pain and sorrow and knew I had to decide. I also knew once I choose, it would be imminent. My spine in pain tingled with the movement of energy willing to shed my bodily temple and move to another realm. I pondered the decision for a time and weighed what I thought were the outcomes, I couldn't move. My brother and greatest friend came to my mind, and also my family, my Mom, and dad, and my younger brother, Matt. I couldn't bear the thought of leaving them here; I felt that if I did, the pain that would result for them would be greater than what I was enduring. I also felt there was something left here on earth for me to do; I have no idea what it is. I chose to stay. When I made the decision, a moment passed and the door for dying was closed and gone. That feeling of being intimate with death so far has never returned. It is so very cumbersome to explain. There is just a knowing that I could, if I chose to, leave my body and drift away from it. A feeling of being able to separate from the body, it is a strange feeling knowing you can leave. The sensation also feels as if it would be permanent. It's somewhat mind-bending!

My injuries were the result of fifteen years of soccer, and other sports as well, but soccer mostly. I used weight training to make up for my small frame and stature and in hindsight this exasperated the problem. My right side was naturally stronger and more responsive and with the weight training it became more pronounced while my left side was in neglect. After my first year of collegiate soccer I tore a ligament on the bottom of my foot leading to the bottom of the heel. I developed plantar fasciitis. Doctors didn't help; I had cortisone shots and elaborate taping schemes but no improvement.

I was forced to sit or limp, so I limped around without putting my left heel to the ground. After three months, my body's compensation caused a chain reaction of disability. My left side was even more weakened and the injury was spreading up my leg to my knee and hip. After five months my hips became so far out of alignment I developed a herniated disc between L4 and L5. The disc pinched nerves across my back, down my leg, up my arm, neck and face. These nerves remained encumbered so long that I began to lose sensation on parts of the left side, along with numbness and hot and cold pockets. I lost motor function in parts of my hand, shoulder, and foot. I would try to move but nothing would happen. I ended up with a severe muscle imbalance and my fascia tears throughout the left side.

My time with Antoinette began the healing process; she marks the moment of reversal. I learned a lot about health and healing and bio-feedback as well as learning how to better attune myself to higher states of being. As a child I had always believed in God but like most people had no tangible perception of what God might be. My identity before her had been solely wrapped around my physical body and its prowess. It was time in my life to change, time to Identify myself with something greater and more encompassing; something truthful and profound, the Great Spirit.

There are many things she said to me that day that I only came to understand or encounter at a later time. The profound ways in which the human consciousness reveals itself is so vast and mysterious; I have yet to scratch the surface in discovering them. In her living room I sat listening to her for over an hour, the session was coming to an end. She asked me to pray with her, she asked me to then look at her which I was already doing. As she prayed I closed my eyes to join her but couldn't stop opening them to look at her while she prayed. I just had to stare at her. Her eyes were closed and I watched such an amazing person. It was a weird way of assessing her and what she was about; I just couldn't keep my eyes closed. She asked the great masters for guidance and clarification then chanted the word aum over and over in a deep melodic tone. I was about five feet away from her on a couch; she was in the middle of the room on a kitchen chair, nothing around her or behind her. She chants. I start to see a hue around her neckline of whiteness. The glow is creeping up behind her as if it is coming from a shower bouncing off her. I can't believe my eyes. I pause and asked myself if this is real or the possibility of some trickery. The light grows and encompasses her whole body but is strongest from the shoulders up around her head. In waves somehow related to my own heartbeat the light pulses out of her, filling the room. The view is like that of blurry heat coming off hot asphalt on a summer street, only it's not clear, it's white, pink, yellow, and turquoise. The white is closest to her body and then blends into soft pink then into yellow or turquoise. I had moments of perfect clarity then shifting to blur and back and forth. Shocked that this was in fact really happening led to fear, I was so amazed that something told me to continue trying to see. As I talked to myself the light would go away, as I focused and concentrated it would come back, so I tried to focus. I felt that

41

this was not a scary thing but something positive and peaceful, I tried to see more. The more I focused the more I could see, I then realized that what I was seeing was truly real, and it was somehow linked to me, I had some influence on it; I could stop it at any time.

I then began to feel warm and serene, special, and comfortable, even though I still was frightened and nervous. This went on for several minutes; I was able to see the aura come through her towards me. She was so bright the background of the room became washed out with light; it was blurry and faded in and out with the light. It was pulsing in waves that seem to get more intense with each pulse then fade again. There were moments when the room was completely gone. I had an image come to my mind; I remember it distinctly and could see it both in my mind and still see the *auric* light of her. The image was tiny specks of orange and white droplets of light that were bouncing off me like I was in a shower. I didn't see the droplet coming on to me but only bouncing off. She now looks bright with pink light around her head and shoulders with turquoise around the pink then white light on the fringes. There is a sense of rhythm with the aura; it's not like a light bulb in your house that is constant. It is pulsating and would come and go in its intensity. The room would fill with light emanating from her, I was mesmerized and feel like I was hardly blinking, I was very still.

Then she spoke and the words came out of her in a voice that hadn't come out of her before. She said deeply and calmly "what are you seeing". I was terrified. The voice was authoritative and deep. I didn't answer, I was in shock again. I also felt that if I spoke or answered I would lose the vision, like it would take a tremendous amount of energy to speak, it was all so hypnotic. I became even more nervous because now the room wasn't fading away but she was. She would disappear in the light and then in a blur reappear. It is not like the room was absent of her but she was just a shape engulfed in a light constantly shifting and pulsating. The light is like the off colors of a photo negative, she was disappearing into some negative space. As she dissolved the only thing that remained of her was her two eyes, floating and piercing me at five feet away, it was eerie. Somehow I still felt protected and that this was not a harmful event.

Her eyes were now beaming, bright blue lights like the reflections off the ocean at peak times of the day. They were amazing and mesmerizing, I couldn't look at anything else, and they had me locked in. I know she was seeing deep into me, my soul. This also scared me to know someone was literally seeing through me. I surrendered to it, at this point I knew whatever was happening it was more powerful than I am, and I hoped it had my best interest in mind. I focused my sight on her penetrating blue eyes, the pulsations continued, she was in and out. As she faded I could see another person where she was, fading in and fading out. There seemed to be a glowing person superimposed onto her. I concentrated. This was definitely no trick. There are no tricks like this available to our realm. I also then realized that I could look away and lose the image and she was just there behind it.

I focused and could see two people shifting over her face. The first one was a man with bold features. He had lots of wavy or curly hair and a blond beard, he seemed handsome. I noticed the beard was very full and very well groomed. His image came and went many times. Then a woman appeared. She seemed older but smiling and bright. I could only really see her face. Her hair was just in the light. It was only her face on top of Antoinette. She faded away and the bearded man came back, I must have looked at them for two minutes or so. It seemed like enough time to really look at their faces and their features. With each pulse they would fade in and fade out but the man stayed the longest. I began to fatigue and slowly the light began to adjust back to normal but I could still see light coming out of Antoinette. It's so odd, its light coming through the eyes or the cheekbones or through the brow, and it makes the facial features more pronounced as they glow. It's like a skeletal structure of light.

She asked me again "what are you seeing" and I told her but had a hard time describing it. I did my best to tell her what I saw, after a few minutes she asked me to walk across the room to the television and look at the photos placed on top. "Do you recognize any of the people"? There were three small pictures there, one of Krishna, one of St. Germain, and one of Jesus. The only one that could possibly resemble was St. Germain, she said: "I thought so; I could feel his presence in the room". I was unsure, the photo looked like a lithograph drawing but it did have similar features, to what I'd seen. She said "our session was ending and whoever they were, they were loving and blessing me". In awe and very tired I thanked her, hugged her and left. She said "we'll see each other again", I knew she was right.

I sat in my car in sheer amazement, I knew my life had changed and would never be the same again. I knew at that moment that the realm of higher spirit and my idea of God did exist. It was a blessing, a confirmation that I assume very few people ever get, I've never doubted the spirit world since. As a child I always knew these things existed but didn't have proof or any way to perceive them. This created tons of questions, many of which are still not answered, but I've not questioned the existence of spirit since.

I drove home to digest and to tell my best friend and older brother my experience. I didn't know how he would react or if he would believe me. My older brother knows me better than anyone on the planet. I have always trusted him and I know he would respond in truth and honesty. The details of my new experience are pouring out to him, he listened intently. I thought I might appear to be crazy but knew what I witnessed was real. He believed me but I was not sure if he believed in the things I saw, he probably never really had a reason to. He lovingly took my story and probed me with questions to which I answered. I could see it in his eyes that he knew I couldn't make something like this up. Time went by and my life changed, my days were filled with my vision, I just obsessed about what I saw and who were the beings I had seen. Do they have an identity, a personality? Eventually I convinced my brother to go to see Antoinette. He was reluctant and I believe a little scared. I insisted he meet her, I needed some conformation about what I went through and I trusted Ian more than anyone. I knew he would again do this for me and he did. I cannot speak for him or his experience, but he did confirm a similar happening. He saw the light and the aura and another being come through. The fact that the person I love and trust most now knew beyond a shadow of a doubt that I was telling the truth was critical to me.

We both knew something greater, higher existed. As time went on I just couldn't get the question of who these beings are out of my mind. I've seen at least five different glowing beings come through her, and I see these things every time I am with Antoinette. My dreams are more interesting as well. The man with the blonde beard has been present every time and none of them have ever spoken to me. I have, on occasion asked them to tell me who they are but to no avail. She tells me I am not in tune with them enough to get more precise information. She tells me to meditate daily; this will help me to vibrate at a higher level and to tune in. I've been able to see auras ever since that day. I can see them if I concentrate, and at times I can feel them as well.

The first session with her I later transcribed on to paper, she tapes each session with a portable tape recorder. I listened to the tape and wrote down most things I felt were of importance. Thinking I could confirm and see if they manifested in the future. In that first session, I was taught many things but the ones I remember most are "the material world is dualistic, and this is an illusion designed to trap the ego consciousness in the material level". She also told me "we don't go to hell, we don't burn, there is no purgatory, these ideas are states of consciousness we can change or manifest". She is a channel and a message bearer for me, and to my knowledge she is the only channel ever to channel known saints. She also told me that she cannot be both a medium and a witness at the same time, so she often only feels the presence of the masters who come through her. A master was said to have an interest in me that day, I know not who or why. I often times question it, why? What do I have to do with all of this? Why is this happening to me? Then I realize how fortunate I am to have seen such things. I am often puzzled and frustrated but I would never have it any other way. "A God realized master can manifest the physical, causal, and astral bodies simultaneously". This means a master has the power to consciously vibrate on all three levels and manifest his presence and control, his purpose:

A soul achieves liberation by the grace delivered from God and by the assistance of the masters.

True avatars have no ego consciousness and never advertise.

The mind can never control the mind.

She has reminded me many times that attunement only comes by way of meditation –

Within the stillness, there is a symphony.
Within the moment, there is eternity.
Within God, indeed there is you,
and within you there is God. – Saint Germain

Five

LIGHT LEADS TO LOVE

Meditation is by far the most fundamental thing that Antoinette has brought into my life. Even though I studied different forms and techniques before we met, my most influential moments started bubbling up once I started practicing the techniques she introduced me to. Please understand I am by no means an authority on mediation and I am only sharing my ideas and experiences. Like most things of profundity, take it with a grain of salt.

The goal is to suspend the thought process and revel in the moments that arise between each thought. As practice creates accomplishment, these moments become longer in duration, until you lose yourself. In essence you have to stop the internal dialogue to begin this journey. Most of us don't realize how present and often the voice inside us speaks or gestures. Even more so, we don't understand that this voice, this inner dialogue is responsible for upholding our perception of reality. Only when someone consciously stops the internal dialogue does this truth reveal itself, so if you don't understand it, then you haven't stopped the dialogue. Placing yourself in the stillness of non-thought is essential to spiritual growth and higher states of consciousness. It's all about expansion. The ideas we have about who, what, and why we are become new and greater than our previous ideas. The word idea when broken into its rudimentary form roughly translates into: *I* - meaning the self/ *dea* - meaning deity or of God. Ideas are our selves recreating ourselves. The mind is limitless, as is our self, as is the universe. When you look out into the sky, or outer space, where do you see its end? You don't, because there is no end. As far as modern science can discern there is really no boundary to the universe. There is no end. It is infinite. So is the self. The limits of the self are self determined. When someone says that there are multiple universes they are misleading by the use of syntax they chose. Once again, the word universe means one verse. So when someone finds a new aspect to the one verse and calls it another universe they are really still referring to the one all encompassing verse, the universe! This is not at all unlike the idea of the monotheistic one God. It's very simple when you think about it. If you believe in one God being all powerful and everywhere at all times, then there is no reason to dispute that God's teachings or authenticity is also present always. The omnipresent God encompasses all things including other names, or versions, or characteristics of other Gods; so your God is but one of the many Gods that make up the one true God. If you see this simple fact then your God has no choice but to accept other versions of itself. Thus there is no need to fight over religious principles. And of course if you believe that your God is love then you must love even the dark and deadly side of things, even the religious beliefs of others.

To know humility is to deny it. It has been said that one cannot be aware of humility. However someone can be aware of vanity. This is a strange paradox that points to the value of parts of the human condition which are out of our control. You can seek to be humble and attain humbleness, but you won't be aware of it at the time. The meditative mind is also known as the seeing mind, meaning the seers of our world see into, and always beyond that which is present. Tricky as this is, it is achieved by being absolutely present. When the mind is totally present it can catch a glimpse of what is new and never before created. Seeing these aspects is what a seer does. They remain tapped into the present universe seeing it as it is created moment by moment, then act to recreate it by the use of their will; easier said than done. Love, like meditation is not cultivated by thought because thought is always based in the past, and love as well as meditation, exist beyond thought, and in the present. Love is tricky, and many people think of love in precepts or concepts which again are all based in thought, and thought is all based on previous thought, so love never arrives. To love, one has to let go of all ideas of love, then allow the new and never before created touch of love to arrive.

Six

TRANSCRIPTIONS

    As we talked, I could see the subtle glow around her head and shoulders. I mostly listened to what she had to say about me. She, Antoinette, was telling me about me. Some of the things she said still today make no sense, while others ring true. On our first meeting, this is what transpired - "A man by the name of Jon wants to make direct contact with you. He wants to show you love and is connected to you from another time, life and place. He is dead, but is looking after you here and now. He wants to see you succeed. Another name comes through very strongly, Scott." She asks: "Do you know a Scott, a close friend or family member?"

"No", I answered.

"The bagpipes and their sound is a strong symbol for you. Meditation is the key to accessing the God force." She said: "You have had a very inventive mind in a past life and unusual mental abilities, a bright mental aspect. You have the ability for creative and abstract thought."

She then instructed me to ask the great masters to see the light of God, the vibration of Christ-Consciousness. I spoke inside my head as instructed: "*(Great masters, please help me to see the light)*". I could see showers of light bouncing off her. "*Your important work in this lifetime is to receive spirituality*", she said. "*All beings are divine children of God and man's journey is the walk of the soul not the body. Perceive nature as condensed light and realize the immortality of the human soul.*"

She said there are problems related to my father with alcohol. She had no idea he has a daily habit. At this time she predicted I would travel to Baja California, the British Isles, Canada, Europe, the Orient, California and Oregon.

There is someone close to me who needs a friend. "His name is Jeff and he is very sensitive. He is so sensitive that he tries to escape his sensitivity and maybe using substance to do it." She says "there is a problem with a woman named Michelle. She and her father have unresolved issues...The mind can never control the mind" she continued. "Through superior techniques of meditation you can consistently move doubt. *Mia Copa Sumahdi*, a blissful state with God."

I am standing on the cliffs of my own understanding, I am awakening. The God force brought me to her and responded to my curiosity. It is aware that I have the potential to awaken early in life. My stream of energy has shifted for all

51

time, and the first meeting will mark a strong significance in my life. Watch out for dead ends on my spiritual journey. The God force wants me to have the opportunity to get spiritual direction. The body is simply a vehicle, a container for the soul. Beware of what others want from me. Ask yourself what do they have to gain from me? Beware of those who want you to surrender your power of Independence of thought. The path of Yogananda ties directly to me.

A true guru is one who's state of consciousness can assist you in your own liberation, and can take you to the place of God realization. She knows and remembers that we at some point shared the energy of God. "Be discriminative while worshiping." She said I had an incarnation where I played music, a stringed or reed instrument. "You have a tendency to not want to be the student, but do affirmations and meditation, and you will have direct guidance from God." I'm receiving inspiration but lack the tools to translate it, I am impatient with myself.

Over time I had many sessions with her and these things we talked about are developing into a more keen awareness of important facets of my life. She said my father may have awkward feelings about not being around for his kids more when we were young. She said my body was not going to have a normal ability to tolerate drugs and alcohol. Many of these transcriptions I will never know fully what their significance is. My father has a real understanding of music and I should work with music whenever I can. There is a significant reason for my tribulations with the body. There are learnings I need to know that come from this; they are changing my consciousness and receptiveness. Whatever I accomplish in the physical form will not be taken beyond the physical form, it will all vanish someday. The only constant in this world is my interrelationship with myself and the God force, everything else will come and go.

She told me where to find and learn superior techniques of meditation. She told me to practice a 20,20,20 breath meditation and learn **aum** energizations. Learn how to move currents in the spine correctly and let no one tell you what scriptures to bring into your life.

On December 13, 2001, my younger brother Matt's 18th birthday, I sat with her. She caused me to think deeply; here is some of what she said: "There are many paths to God realization and there is truth in great souls. An avatar is basically karma free when it decides to incarnate on earth. A soul's teachers will change according to the soul's state of consciousness and evolution. When a soul's goal becomes liberation only the assistance of the God chosen guru (dispeller of darkness) master can help to work out the intricacies of karma. A God-realized master can manifest the physical, causal, and astral bodies simultaneously. Only by attunement to the great masters can (I) attain liberation." I feel I am surrendering my will to the will of God, but somehow I don't understand that the feeling is still ego based. I have a strong tendency to go astray, on mental journeys. This is keeping me from liberation. She told me she has experienced on two occasions the merging with the breath of Christ at the Crucifixion; the crown, the wounds, and the stigmata appeared upon her. Think about that! This holy person is sharing these insights with me. I am still dumbfounded, and pondering all that it means.

Nothing can come into manifestation without first being in thought. – **Antoinette Spurrier**

One day in La Jolla, California I sat with her again. As usual the feeling of love and compassion radiated from her. By now I knew she was a good spirit and I was really no longer skeptical. I just have trusted her since all the things she has guided me in have worked out in a positive way. I still have the problems in my lower back and left side, however after doing as she instructed, I have been making great and steady progress, so I kept going. It would be some five years or so before the back issues really settle into a full recovery and much longer to balance the myofascia of the left side.

She told me I have an unusual ability with bodily coordination and this is why athletics have been natural to me. She goes on. "Everyone cannot just decide to do or be something, and make it happen, it takes time and focus. What is common for all souls is that they are divine children of God, and many people don't realize this. Nothing can go into manifestation without first being in thought, from the causal comes the light realm. The material realm is made of opposites, like cause and effect, like attraction and repulsion. Man forgets his divine nature while playing in creation. If we remember our divinity we can never be lost from God. In the east, the basic thought is that man is always going to make mistakes until he reawakens to the memory that he is divine. And human conduct will remain unreliable until man is anchored in the light of God, the divine. This is really the nature of sin. Sin is not evil, just ignorance. The process of self-realization believes that man only ceases to make mistakes by awakening.

I was instructed to use cold pressed peanut oil on my stiff joints, my back, and lubricate the tendon daily. Also she taught me to use castor oil packs over the left side of my abdomen. Make a small barrier layer out of plastic wrap. This keeps the oil from getting all over the heating pad. Put the castor oil directly on a piece of uncolored flannel and place it two inches away from the navel on the left side. The heated oil is good for the lymphatic system, helps the glands, and boosts the immune system. For the first two weeks do it every day for at least an hour and a half. After that do three days on, four days off, for at least two months. It takes one month to penetrate the lymphatic system.

I was doing all kinds of remedies suggested by her, I don't know which ones work for sure, but I did get better. I used fenugreek tea, shark cartilage, apple cider vinegar, Hatha yoga, blue green algae, geranium, multivitamins and more. She said that I am impatient with myself, and I expect to have things mastered much too quickly; first learn to walk then learn to run. The spiritual path and progress dominates all other endeavors in this life. All things will eventually have to be let go of.

The drama of the body often happens to a soul who's ready to awaken into spiritual consciousness. For me this drama will have to be played out for advancement in healing as well as the spirit. "The identification with the physical body is being taken away and only happens to a soul of higher advancement. It means it is time to discover your soul". She gave me an affirmation to heal the body, "I give thanks to God for the miraculous healing of my body now. I am whole. I am healed. I am radiant in God's healing light. I exist in a state of divine bodily perfection". I still use this affirmation today.

She went on to tell me of how she used to be a dancer and a good one. She loved it with all her heart, as I love my sports of surfing and soccer. She explained the painful mourning over the loss of her physical body when it was taken away from her. Her passion can no longer be fulfilled by the graceful movement of the physical body. How depressing and painful it is to lose such a vital part of yourself. In return, her clairvoyant and healing gifts were bestowed upon her. She understands her spiritual role now in this life, this is her purpose here. She can no longer dance, and when you see her you know this, but the many lives she has touched is immeasurable. Her gift to mankind is incredible. I know I am blessed to have her in my life. There is that which is within that is untouchable by pain.

She says that we are never the roles we play out. The spirit is asking who are you, who is it that thinks you are this role? What are you, who is the thinker? Who is the force behind this thought? The lesson is you are more than the roles you play. There is something behind these roles that is immutable, beautiful, and divine. Life is a succession of the stripping away of identity. The higher self will continue to attract the adversity that will force you to ask yourself "Who is behind the role your playing?" You know an instrument by that which flows through it. God can force anything upon you except he can't force you to love him.

Go to the power of mediation no matter what religious affiliation you are inclined to. Keep the techniques consistent this will make the biggest difference in your life. The more you meditate, the better your ability to extract the core meaning of things. There is truth in all religions and their ultimate goal is a personal one, to attune the individual to God. I came to her because the flowering of consciousness is occurring in me.

My family and I have had spiritual experience with her, and this is not true of everyone who sees her. It strikes me oddly that my brother Ian and my mother Mary also had paranormal experiences with her. Mary James, wife of Bob James, was sitting with Antoinette after hearing my story. She had made an appointment to see her knowing she would be in California visiting her sons. I felt so blessed that she peered into the auric light as well. It is so special that she understands the impact this has had on me. I was also responsible for disrupting her moments in the light; I rattled on the door while she was in the aum vibration. I came to pick her up and needed to make it to work on time. How I wish I would have waited just a few minutes more, and not pulled her away from such a mystery. My mother is the reason I am able to even write this book, I love her with all my heart as she is the one person who has never stopped believing in me; and having that in my life has revealed itself to be critical for my well being. She has taught me that each and every person needs, and deserves the same to make it in this world! I would not be half the man I am without her.

There will come a day when I must leave this body behind. My injury and its drama were meant to throw me into spirit. Destiny is ultimately tied to spirit. The only way to internalize consciousness is through meditation.

Live by the spirit, and the spirit will live in your life.

If you identify with spirit you will never forget the process the soul makes in this incarnation. It is the only identification that won't let you down. Loyalty to oneself and your individual truth is the highest law. There is a point where the self can't grasp where it is going, when it can't see the end destination. It's okay, don't wait for intellectual understanding. Just rely on the techniques of attuning to God. Affirmations turn the energy of the universe toward your thoughts, they create magnetism.

Seven

THE WITHERING

The withering feeling of my body dying is present while stretching from the core to heal. Lying on the floor in my memory, in my mind; this state brought on by the meditative quality of severe stretching. I put in countless hours of stretching, so much I dare try to figure out how long I've stretched parts of my body to chase a sensation of relief. The muscles are not the problem. Over the years I've realized the myofascia is the culprit, the stubborn one. I can put the body into a

58

position and put weight on it to stretch a fiber for hours. Usually about two hours at a time for one position. When you do this you either think, or distract yourself with a movie, or some sort of mental daydream, but you can't sleep. I've tried to sleep, only to wake up with numbness and loss of circulation.

When you're asleep the consciousness needed to direct and put energy into the body part is gone. The strangeness is strange to say the least. How I wish I could just use gravity and posture to stretch. It would be much easier. You must remain awake and focused. It almost demands your attention. It becomes a lesson in attention and its power. Attention directed correctly generates biofeedback, the mind body relationship. Without attention the body seems to become quite literally asleep. With attention the body responds to thoughts, sounds, internal dialogue, and visions in the mind's eye. That being said, still years of focused attention have been needed to elicit the smallest measure of progress. I feel the myofascia moving but it is fiber by fiber. It is like a steel braided cable and your task is to stretch it and loosen it to the position of best balance in the body. One fiber releases to reveal the next weakest, and so on. Millions of tiny fibers contract and constrict based on the mind state, level of fatigue, concentration, and what you eat and drink that day.

The complex and tedious task of healing such a problem is monumental. I've made great strides and seen so much progress that I know to push on. I know balance will be mine some day. Also, the nature of such an illness without stretching the body becomes arthritic and twisted and stiff. It basically tells me when I need to stretch. I therefore am obsessed and addicted to the exercise. On some level it is biofeedback reminding me of my progress and my work to be done. Some of the sensations that occur are incredible both in pain and pleasure. It was difficult to know how far to push the body the first couple of years, due to new types of pain. The release of areas of the body is amazing and liberating. The body wants to be well and yearns for such healing. A lot of this injury is hidden deep in the psyche and directly corresponds to the spiritual state one is in. The karmic ties as they are worked out and transcended, reveal new conscious states that in turn reflect and reveal new body states. Our emotional, mental, and spiritual health manifests the physical health.

It's tough to describe the feeling of withering away from the core of your being. I believe it is the touch of death, the life force leaving the body. It's similar to your body not responding to your mind and thoughts, very frustrating. It's like a plant with no minerals or water to draw up its stem. The dryness makes things brittle and withers into just a shell that eventually crumbles. It is such an odd feeling, a "disconnect" from what is natural and lifelike. You wilt from the inside of your energy, your chi is like the river flowing to the sea diverted to a side pool with the tiniest tributary keeping the connection to the main flow. You feel the life water drying up in your soul; scary. Then you scream and cry for a flood of rain from the gods, and hope your waters reach the mighty sea once again.

So I found myself planning, and embarking on what could be the vacation of a life time. The reason this trip is so special is because my brother and closest friends are all accompanying me, something that took a lot of logistical genius to make happen. We are all off to the lush and lively country of Panama. Surfing is the main point of such a trip. I love the warm water, friendly people, and uncrowned waves. My brother makes this special as well because we rarely get to travel together. I am ready for the adventure of a lifetime, and all those I care about most are right there with me. Bam! Halfway through the excursion, my lower back gives out. Just a wrong move and the pain is debilitating. The worst thing on a surf trip is injury. All my pals are psyched out of their gourds and I am lying around searching for ibuprofen, needless to say it sucked. Not the trip, but the frustration of still having back pain and problems after thirteen years.

The overall adventure ended up good enough, put in about half the trip in the water, catching waves, but with the stiffness of an admiral's salute. Cambutal has some amazing point breaks and captivating coastline. I hope to see it again someday, hopefully before I am too old and decrepit to surf. Back at home in California, and back to work, my back is still agitated. It is improving but slowly. After a great massage from Julianna Bruni, who is an incredible therapist, I begin to feel better. That night I slept so deep and peaceful. The next day, after a tough day at work, I lay down on a round, foam roller. This roller is designed to stretch and decompress the spine. I had been using it on and off for a few months. I hold it right on my lower back and I can feel the tightest part of my spine begin to respond. It feels like the space between the vertebrae is being slowly pulled apart. I had some intense sensations after about fifteen minutes: hot, then cold, undulations, pulses, and pain, also some relief. I concentrated on the pain, and repeated a healing mantra in my mind.

I bring light into the body through the back of my head at the medulla oblongata. Then mentally place it in the spine where I need healing. I do this for just over an hour. The stretch is so intense and draining, but I can feel progress so I keep going. It feels like I am stretching the myofascia around the muscles. It's like stretching one fiber at a time, and when one fiber relaxes another tightens. I have been stretching my entire body for about fifteen years and still having extreme tension in certain places. All my friends are boggled. They think I am one of the healthiest people they know, but I am still in pain. It's like the spine is crunchy and not smooth and moist, such a frustrating injury. It gets so intense I want to quit but I can't. It's the most release I've had at one time ever, so I have to let it settle itself to see if I can gain progress. I eventually do, but the level of intensity is piercing. I can't even move enough to get off the foam roller. After an hour the tension subsides and the blood begins to flow back into the spine. I see lights in my mind, just like when you close your eyes real tight. I creep off the roller and lie on the floor. It takes ten minutes or so before I can sit, and then stand.

I stand with a stale footing, I feel closer to being centered. I feel more balanced than I have in fifteen years, it's a monumental victory, and there is still more to battle. I just hope this one leads to another victory and that it doesn't take years to accomplish. I am obsessed with reversing the withering, even if I have to do it one fiber at a time, but I pray...please not just one frustrating fiber at a time!

Eight

First Lodge

The opening of awareness is now on the forefront of my mind. For years now I have been searching for answers. Answers to major questions: Who are we? Why are we here? Am I really infinite? What is the nature of God? Well, nothing has changed. I still don't know the answers. I am now into my second year of daily meditation and seeing some profound results. All kinds of experiences, some mystical, others humbling, and others elating. The perspective on life changes into something new, and that, in itself is liberating.

Tide and the Crannog

I must be ready for, and prepared for something new, another process, another way to sharpen my intent. I've always felt a deep respect and admiration and kinship for the Native American spiritual tradition. Since I was a boy I wanted to be an Indian, not a cowboy. The Indian was stronger, more self reliant, and wiser than any other American. My relationship with nature just reinforced my desire to learn more about the Amerindian. With vigor and determination I searched for a sweat lodge in the deserts of southern California. It was no easy task. It took time to learn about them through research and books, as well as find one that would accept me.

The first lodge was eye opening to say the least, the process itself is opening.

One does not become enlightened by imagining figures of light, but by making the darkness conscious. – Carl Jung

I drove to my father's house in the California dessert, Morongo valley. From there the lodge was about twenty more minutes away. I stopped for a light dinner and talked with my dad. He and I have always understood each other on a spiritual level. He, in his day, explored in many ways the opening up of oneself. He primarily used his creativity through musicianship and craftsmanship to unload his creativity. With thirty five years of playing music as a lifestyle he managed to tap into the astral world in multiple ways. He has always been the one who understood my questions about the nature of the universe, self, and mind. He has experienced these same paranormal events that I have, and am now questioning.

He supported me with ease and respect, he seemed to know what I was about to encounter. He encouraged me and would wait for my return. The night air was crisp and the sky was dark. Stars were peering into the little town. The desert at night is charged with wonderment in its energy. I was nervous as I drove to the house. I had only spoken to the lodge leader by phone, we had never met.

Tide and the Crannog

I arrived, walked to the door and was greeted by a portly woman. She directed me around back where I saw the fire blazing and a small group of people sitting around, quietly talking.

I introduced myself, everyone was friendly. I respectfully greeted the leader and asked for basic guidance about the procedure. It was my first time in a sweat lodge. He was a chubby white man with a gray beard and kind eyes. He gave me a lesson about the four directions, their meaning, and corresponding colors. He told me the way to approach the dome structure, which way to walk around it, to pray to each direction, and enter on my hands and knees. Before this happened I chatted with the others, mostly polite small talk. There was time to kill as the lodge was getting prepared and the fire was tended too. When it was my turn to begin, I took my clothes off and just left a pair of shorts on. I prayed to each of the four directions, moved around the lodge clockwise, put a pinch of tobacco into the fire and asked for clarity about my path in life. A man smudged me from head to toe, and front to back with a coffee can full of burning sage and an eagle feather. The sweet smell immediately put me at ease, I felt calm and peaceful. The smoke cleanses the body before entering the sacred lodge, which represents the womb of the earth. He fanned that smoke all over me with the eagle feather. Just before I entered, the leader told me that once I go in there, there is no leaving until the ceremony is finished. He then told me once I enter; the outside world is forever changed. I crawled in, took my spot in the west end, the spot of seeking for an answer. The west symbolizes the place where rain comes from. Its associative color is black. The darkness is where things come to an end, west and its power is the end, the finality of things.

We prayed in there and the hot rocks from the fire were brought in one by one, each causing the lodge to get hotter. After many stones, our grandfathers are brought in, the door is closed and there is water poured over the stones. Dry herbs are sprinkled on them creating the sweetest and hot sensation in my nose. The smell of burning cedar and lavender bolted me into a memory of when I was a child. No particular memory just the feeling of looking at the joys of the world through a child's eyes. It was beautiful. With each dowsing the stones ejected hissing heat at you, you cannot escape. It is oppressive to say the least. All this goes on with singing, drumming and praying. There is nothing like it I've ever felt. My lungs filled with steaming hot air, and I am fearful but high from the smells. My body beads up sweat and my insides come oozing out with rain pouring down my face from the crown of my head. I am forced to keep my composure by being forced to meditate. My body is telling me to run and get out, but I vowed to stay no matter what happened. I was so nervous.

I remember opening and closing my eyes and seeing absolutely no difference, there is only darkness. I sensed myself all over the top of the lodge, I was expanding. The sense that I was no longer contained by my body was unfolding, and as time went on I felt I could sense and perceive things outside the lodge. I opened my eyes and salty hot sweat filled them up. I closed my eyes and my attention focused on my third eye. I began to feel at peace after the first round was over. They opened the door and let cool air rush in over you, a wanted break. Each round got harder and more intense, there were four all together. In the third and fourth rounds I began to see blue and orange sparks in the lodge. My eyes were open. I knew there was no light in there. Still I saw mostly orange sparks and trailing lights right in front of me. I watched them popping around for many minutes. It was mesmerizing. These lights were not lighting up the lodge. I could still not see other people around me. They were not brightening the space I was in, but were surely flashing right in front of my face. I took this experience as a good omen. I made it through to its completion, and made some quick friends. The songs in the Lakota language still ring in my heart, they were bold and powerful. I don't know what the words meant, but the inflection and tone still resonate with me today. I pray to Tunkashila because of this, on a regular basis. Tunkashila is the grandfather of all grandfathers and grandmother is the Earth.

I was calm and clearheaded for days after the lodge. I was happy and peaceful. I went on to participate in more lodges from time to time, each one different and revealing. They would go on to reveal parts of myself to myself and through the forced meditation I can sense myself slowly becoming. I believe the Native Americans were, and are more in tune with the human aspect connected to our planet than many modern societies. They know what they are doing. Just study the Sundance ceremony and you'll learn of the tremendous commitment they have to spirit. I hope to someday be of that stature. The uses and tools employed are committed to God now, today, not some promise of heaven that never arrives. They see how to deal with liberation here and now. You either are ready or you're not. If you are not, then you must cultivate that readiness in ways that suit you; but if you are ready, the natives will bring you face to face with your liberation.

I, myself, apparently am not ready. Let's jump forward to my fourth lodge.

I am already given the power that rules my fate.
And I will cling to nothing, so I will have nothing to defend.
I have no thoughts, so I will see.
I fear nothing   so I will remember myself.
Detached and at ease I will dart the eagle to be free.
– Carlos Castaneda

The location of my fourth lodge was in Dalzura, California. I enjoyed the small Rocky Mountains and blue skies. The morning came like a smack in the face, abruptly awake and already late. The feeling of drunkenness from deep sleep wore off as the traffic angered my attention. Making wrong turns and cursing at the lack of signage, I made it to the lodge and felt I must have missed the opening lesson. I walked up and the Amerindian with the shovel looked at me and said "slow down, you're on time. Slow down because that is what this day is all about". Not knowing anyone, I introduced myself to a few people, and with a little small talk we all sat and waited while the pit was dug. The rocks were carefully selected. The fire was built into a pyramid of wood, stones, and shavings. The sun burned my back and chest. As the two hours or so passed with a lesson in Native American Inipi ceremony blended with credible philosophy. As we were smudged I said good bye to this world and entered my fourth sweat lodge.

The lack of personal space made it difficult to get comfortable. The door closed with the grandfathers hissing their presence. The waves of heat came on fast. I was used to this, I had done this before. This is what I told myself. The waves became so intense so fast I knew I had to focus and the battle began. My heart was pounding with each drumbeat, bubbles of sweat bounce off my chest. My mind was telling me to get out of there, that I couldn't breathe. I was telling my mind to stay in there, I could do it. All I could hear of my own voice was my own little chant "I can do it, I can do it". But something else was telling me that I couldn't breathe and I was going to faint. This went on faster and faster, so fast that I couldn't keep track of what was being said. I hear a man in the lodge scream under his breath "suffocation, suffocating". The ball of panic was in my upper stomach and no oxygen was there, only fear. Ironically it wasn't fear of death, it was just fear itself.

I spoke out but didn't tell myself to speak. My voice just leaped out of me, "I have to get out of here, I have to get out". "I am sorry, I am sorry" as I crawled to find the door that I knew was to my right. I climbed by others who were singing Lakota prayer songs and drumming. As I hear the lodge leader Dan Moon say "Open the door," the fire tender put his hand on my shoulder and said "don't leave, you're alright, just lie down". The light from the day creeps in and I can't hold myself up anymore. I am on all fours but collapsing, shaking profusely. The words of the fire tender (Grey Bear) made it to my mind. "Lie down, just lie down". Cool water trickled on the crown of my head, such a relief. With my head being poured upon and my back and spine being poured upon, I submitted and lay down. My head just out of the door and my body still in, exhausted, embarrassed. I had stopped the ceremony for everyone involved.

All I could see with my perception of fatigue was the grainy dirt in my face and a blue flip-flop Grey Bear placed for my head. The flip-flop was drenched in my sweat, saliva, and soil. I was picturing myself lying on my stomach with both arms folded into my chest, not able to move anything but my eyes. Seventeen other people I had just met two hours earlier watching and praying. A few minutes of complete exhaustion passed and then I was questioned privately outside the lodge, my energy almost totally gone. The leader stared at me calmly and asked his questions. I remember very little of what was said. I felt like he was talking in slow motion and I could only hear tones coming from him.

I was told to finish the remaining three rounds. I drank lots of water and laid myself down in the lodge and put some soaked wet sage in my mouth. I finished the ceremony with the smell of sage and pounding drums. One ear was hearing the drum next to my head, and the other hearing the drum coming back to swallow me through the earth. My chest was face to face, quite literally with the salt of mother Earth. I learned a valuable lesson that day:

Anything can be accomplished with the correct focused energy!

This would become the first lesson in my personal code of life. The code I take with me that teaches me how to live.

We humans are just reflections of a more powerful consciousness. We are the blinking, glistening lights reflected on the ripples of the ocean. We see ourselves and our patterns on those shiny days when the luminaries flash on and off. (This is apophenia.) Each new ripple is a new incarnation as we make our journey to the shore. We lap upon the sand with our last stretched energy and reach a place never before reached as we disintegrate back into the ocean we never left.

Nine

HEART

Waiting for the mind to know what the heart already knows; I am so busy with the mind that I am not listening to the heart, I am blocked.

Increase devotion and meditation and you will know.
– Antoinette Spurrier

The heart leads and rules us more than we may know or want to believe. As we spend all our time using the intellect and the mind, it grows strong as does the ability to dissect and criticize. The heart also has a knowing, it has an energy that combines with our intuition to lead us. The problem is learning to hear and listen to it.

If you live your life without considering what your heart is telling you then there will come the day when your dreams are dashed away. You will be left with all your intellectual property all around you, but will still yearn for happiness. Happiness is found in the whole being, it is found in the center of our heart's desire. The truth of this is directly related to our core desire to be loved. All those who deny or don't recognize this will someday face it. The love of your friends, and family, and spouses will be what you remember as you leave this life. When dying is at hand all smarts and possessions lose their value because they are of the material world; what is in your heart is of the spiritual world. All our ups and downs in life prepare us to open the heart to love.

A special stimulus comes to the heart, I think, from our outer environment; with time the outer stimulus or energy probes us to become, to grow. Then the stimulus becomes a kind of curiosity to know the stimulus itself. Then we want to know the stimulus well enough to influence it consciously. When you influence it consciously then you gain real aspiration to change into something new, to create. You can place your touch into something never before seen. It's what every single person wants. This cradles a spark in us that will always push us forward. Creativity then looks at the outer environment and makes a reflection of it. The reflection is then changed by the absorbing inner environment, the self. Now the inner environment has a reflection within it, and uses the reflection's energy to produce the power to look outside once again for more stimuli. This connects the life outside to the life inside.

The best life to absorb would be the one you naturally absorb without generating any excess energy or stress. This life is communication, progress, and invigoration. This life is inspiration; and inspiration is the only thing that gives energy to create, and we create once again this life.

Tide and the Crannog

Somehow it was created, a path with heart, a selfless force. Also created was a selfish force. When they collide and communicate, man is born. The creation has manifested in a variety of substance which bleed into one another when close. The earth, its fire, air, water, proteins and salty chemicals will constantly affect and change each other. Some will change through giving, others through talking. Still a new blood will be born. These events compile, thus causing distance and time to exist. Through time, events or actions move toward the stars and their solidarity consists of remaining still light. As a planet bleeds and becomes light, some life energy will be spared due to not being bright enough and ready. The people/ spirits that can hold the silence of love, and be as still as light, become a star. Those that vibrate dimly flee the bright planet and travel to another one that needs more light. People always realize the earth is the life that the stars shine for. They feel alone in the stars until more dim light arrives through the ether of ancient spirits, showing them that the distance of people through space is a bright dance of love.

The heart is God, the divine self, the divine reality. The realization of the heart is fully conscious awakening as the self existing and self-radiant transcendental, and inherently spiritual divine being and person. Divine self-realization is associated with the opening of the primal psycho-physical seat of con-sciousness and attention in the right side of the heart; Hence the term (the heart) for the divine self. One who is awake as consciousness (even in the witness position) generally becomes sensitive to the current of spiritual energy associated with the occasion of the chest, and he or she feels the mind, or attention, falling into its point of origin there. – Adi Da

What is meant by this is that the sensation of God, the divine, or spirit, is no longer a separate awareness; the awareness of the divine is no longer that of the witness. Both your heart and the Great Spirit are the same non-dual reality, you become and are your own natural truth.

Ten

QUESTIONS

I met with the seer/channel/clairvoyant/yogi again. I go through the tapes recorded during our sessions and I write down anything of significance, anything I feel is important to me. The process is supposed to get my questions answered, but I am not sure that it does. I often see the process unfolding and creating more and more questions. I do manage to come to some worthy conclusions though.

As the light comes through her I experience the room filling with light, that is my perception, but what happens on her end, I wonder?

"*Ryan*", she says, "*There is more than one meaning or significance to the witness. I get relatives or close friends coming through. It's not always a saint or master. Some people have seen me as a child and in all stages of my life. The spirit doesn't tell me all the answers either. Somehow the time/space continuum is altered and the past will often appear in the present. I am not always aware of when it is happening. I am not always aware of when the spirit is coming through. The gift comes through integrity. Those that have had gifts in previous incarnations claim the rights to those gifts in another.*"

"*The soul knows the connection when it is ready, even though it gets buried in the unconscious. The bearded man you most often see could be yourself, as you said he resembles you, or it could be someone that had a strong connection with you in a past incarnation. I have no control over the gift. It is just another dimension of God. There was a man who counted and tracked twenty-four entities he witnessed here through the gift. The last one he saw was Anadamoi, an extraordinary saint from India.*"

"*I am a spiritual intuitive on the yogic path. Spirit descends into matter. The sequence of descending is formlessness into initial thought, to light vibration, then to the physical vibration. It goes from formlessness to causal, to astral, to material. The earth and planets are not really self aware like man is. The planet has consciousness and intelligence but no karma or soul. The Earth can show you God in nature but it can't show you realization.*"

"*There are wonderful lines of teachers in many cultures, and the bottom line is what path gives you connection to spirit, and access to inner peace. Through superior techniques of meditation, if you genuinely apply them you will chart your progress. Ask yourself are you happier? Does it result in positive changes in yourself? Then stay with that path. If God was a mountain then there would be more than one path up to the top. But for each soul walking, there is only one path up for them. If you're walking a path that has heart, then you somehow make it."*

I asked more and more questions: "Antoinette, since the soul is said to be eternal, is the soul deathless? Is it birth-less?"...

"The soul somehow became created as an individualized aspect of God. God was formless before he became form, and a true guru is one who knows the past history of a soul. The true guru has to know everything about a soul in order to assist in liberation of the soul. Animals have no karma, they are self aware but not to the extent of creating karma. It is at the point when we are in human form that we begin to take on karma. The importance of a true guru in liberation occurs when a life form begins to acquire karma and begins to use free will."

She went on: *"The spirit doesn't usually let me know of his interest in someone, but Yogananda did reveal to me he has a special interest in you, he has a higher tie to you with the great masters. I believe in you and don't ever doubt that God has single-handedly chosen this lifetime for you to have the ability to do his work. Go forward and claim God, nothing can be higher for a soul."*...

"What do you feel or see when the light is coming through you?" I asked.

"It is important to know that when a being comes through the light, it is never random. It is connected to that soul and has a purpose. The light is a doorway that many want to make contact through to the earth plane. But it is the God-force that regulates who gets through and who doesn't. Only the beings deemed important for the soul will get through. When a master comes over me I rarely know who it is, I always expected I would know, but that is not the case. I feel a pulling in my upper spine when Swami Sri Yukteswar works with me, that's how I know it's him. I get an intuitive feeling most of the time, but it is hard to discern always who is coming through."

"I believe that there is a final path tied to our liberation, but that doesn't mean that that path is the only experience we will have, nor does it mean that we haven't known many other masters before."

She told me that when we first met she had a feeling that Yogananda had orchestrated my coming to her, and that his role with me was vital. Most of the time she is not in a place of knowing but sometimes Yogananda is around. She feels he is always there and around her, but not necessarily present in the room.

"God brings souls from all different paths to me and I don't know my role or why."

She went on to tell me about others who have seen, relatives, friends, children, Christ, the Buddha and other saints come through her. She is the conduit, a channel that some can attune to. There is no doubt in my mind she is the most holy person I've ever met.

A few weeks later I was reading and stumbled on a book of which I don't recall the title. This book was talking about free writing to access your sub-conscious mind as a form of meditation. I was not really very interested in this, but had plenty of free time that day. I read the instructions and did it, here is what came out:

> *"It is coming to be that in the future your thoughts and channels are going to change through the good people that you meet. Give them the blessings they deserve and let them know you love them. If they love you then so be it. If they want to end you then so be it. If they want you to be something special then they are something special. Don't judge them for anything at all. If they are your true friend then they may become special to you in the past, present, and future. Let it slide like a river current in the mist of shadows in the lane beyond all trees in bloom. Come to be the love of all things present. While you are present give thanks and praises to daily life. Along the path you will see signs or directions and they will lead you to salvation in the*

midst of the storms. Go to the end if you must but don't let the end go to you. You are all in life, and be pliable. In the way you do your work take the less than equal posture in the middle of the road. Your natural skill as the mediator is something you can be. Write when you want to write, sing when you want to sing, and play when it is time to play. Don't put any limits on anything because there are no limits. Limits don't exist. When they come up they are figurative in a way that we don't understand. If you can be all there is in the land of your dreams, then you are the dream and have come to real reality."

Eleven

Man In Love

Witches and queens haunt and hug most men's lives. I don't pretend to know the way other men really feel about their love for a woman. It is among the most personal and mysterious aspects we embody. With both witches and queens we are spurred on to learn, but in truth witches can be deadly for a man. For a man to survive a real witch he must be centered and strong or else she will crush his spirit and taste for love. Be keen and wise to detect a witch and stay away. On the other side of things is the mystery of a queen, or even a women on her way to becoming one; there are many stages to go through. The mysterious ways of a loyal, respectful, and honest woman are immeasurable. There is nothing better, nothing sweeter!

The last time I loved a true and respectable woman was the last woman who believed in me. My memories percolate; be without, oh this is when I find what I am with. When she is gone, again there comes the absence. It is indescribable and not forceful, being without. To speak is to limit and box a feeling we don't comprehend. She casts spells and not with words. She casts spells that keep us together when I am not with her, and again I am left with expression that will not word. If I could speak it, it would be so rash and become written in ink, soot or symbol. Maybe if someone else read it they would call it a heart shape. Curved is my mind, my intent, and it even travels wave-like. Her shadows are delighted and I see them in photographs. They are hugging her always, even in the dark. If my eyes water and rush over rocks to touch a softness only known to women, it is not against her. I feel of course to drive a course set by imagined points in an empty space. There I cannot survive the soothing smells of her softness. She is soothing and shredding the debris that we try to stick to ourselves, she will sooth me.

Twelve

DREAMING

At morning I dreamt of you, as I slept in a strange world. There I was laid out as a horizontal where my perception and function change. I move as a fluid with obscure identity and not as a vertical reaching for the sky. A hole over my head; drops down a pigeon next to my slumber. I see you outside and throw the bird to you. It dives into your hands; please receive! Now it falls through your hands to the ground. It falls to sacred ground where you stand, where you are, where your scent dwells.

Tide and the Crannog

This day I awoke with the immediate and vivid memory of that bird in the dream just earlier leaving my hands as I threw it to her. What does it all mean? Only the dreamer knows for sure. The dream stuck with me. I found myself thinking about it days later because of its intensity and feeling of actually happening. There are all kinds of symbols and metaphors said to reveal the truth about dreams but here in this dream, I am attuned to the mystical emotion felt in the dream state. This emotion is where I want to be to find my understanding.

Intuitively I see her (Antoinette) as my guide and guardian whom I desperately want to receive my gift (the bird). I must be seeking her approval and don't yet have the wisdom to approve things for myself. She catches it but lets it fall threw her hands to the ground. The ground where the holy stands is sacred and imbued with spirit. At her feet my winged gift sits as my feathered appreciation for all she has done for me in this life.

The dream world has its claws in consciousness just as does the waking world. So just because we sleep doesn't negate the reality of the dream world. Science has much evidence to prove that the mind cannot distinguish between what it sees inside with eyes closed, and what it sees outside with eyes open. The mind is active and participating in the dreaming, as well as influencing it. The trick is to consciously influence the dream world. When you can influence and design your dream world, whatever powers you cultivate there can bleed over into your waking world. However the dream world has a different set of laws and physics than the waking world, so some translations mutate or simply break-down. Still the personal power gained in either realm is yours to keep and command. This is what Carlos Castaneda delineates in his book entitled The Art of Dreaming.

I just think that most people refuse to be open to such things so they don't exist for them. There was a time when the idea of the earth being round was preposterous; today the flat earth is preposterous. If we can open up to mental capabilities then oddly enough, they begin to reveal themselves. It is said, and in some documented cases that certain aboriginal tribes teach, practice, and use telepathy as an everyday form of communication. They have this skill built into their family life and culture. So from an early age children develop this part of themselves and the appropriate part in their minds. To these aboriginals, telepathy is not unlike body language, only it is more subtle and sophisticated. These are categorized as psychic powers, but maybe these are just highly developed sensitivities of the human being. After all, we are among the only self-conscious beings on the planet.

Upon waking one morning, I instantly had the full memorization of the dream I either just had, or had earlier that night. It was just rushing through my waking mind, and I am typically a slow riser in the morning. I come out of very deep sleep like a bear comes out of a successful hibernation. The rush was so vivid, fast, and intense that I knew I had to write it down, so I did. I had been reading up on dreams and dreamlike states of consciousness and recalled a friend of mine, Dr. John Harris telling me that all the things and caricatures in our dreams are really just us. I applied that philosophy to my current dream and without a doubt it brought the events into a clear picture. Thinking this way causes me to wonder about the nasty, creepy, and horrible characters in some of my dreams; are these immoral creatures really just an extension of myself? Am I capable of such grotesque thoughts and actions? The idea does make a lot of sense because the dream is generated from my own mind so all that's in the dream stems from me somehow. I know I've beaten, killed, maimed, seduced, fornicated, loved, hated, cried, and laughed in the dream world. Apparently I did all this to myself.

There seems to be an on-looking voice at times in the dream world. The voice guides and directs me to make decisions and take action. The dream voice is a deeper part of me, more in tune with the subconscious, more in tune with my true self. However if that voice is ever evil or demonic then I would say there is a problem. I've never experienced such things, but I have read about cases like this. Carl Jung also agrees with this idea of it all being a part of yourself, it is essentially the same idea as the collective consciousness. However to what extent our dreaming body has access to the collective dreaming body I am not sure, but there are cases all over the world of multiple people experiencing the same dreamscape, at the same time, which makes sense, just as many people experience the same waking state at the same time. Remember though that everyone's experience of reality is unique unto themselves.

The dream I wrote down that day was in a house. It was totally unique, but still had qualities of a childhood neighbor's house I used to play at a lot, from the porch to the inside stairway. Upstairs in a house looking in the bathroom mirror I saw a glowing bird-woman. She was in the mirror behind me but somehow actually inside the mirror. She was looking at me, but not behind me, she was dwelling in the mirror itself. She is recognizable, I know her as Antoinette. She is older and thinner and luminous. I tried to yell or say something to her and then left quickly. I was scared, but not petrified. I was more anxious.

As I was halfway down the stairs I found I couldn't talk in whole sentences, I could only mumble. I tried to call for my mother. "Mom!" I knew she was in the house, downstairs. I froze, I found myself halfway down the stairs lying on my back trying to yell, "Mom!" but could only get out low mumbles. She heard me and came to me, and asked "What did you see?" I said I wasn't sure, but I thought I saw another being, or a different type of being. She said that she had been hearing them lately. I asked where? She looked at me intently and said she had been hearing them on the radio, then made a gesture with her face and eyes that pointed to the sky. She said she considered them as darkness and thoughtless, or unthoughtful. I found myself awake in my bed, and I was talking. I was saying a peculiar phrase, "Walk through the valley of the shadow of death."

I still don't know what the significance of this dream means. I see it as a kind of metaphor for the space between worlds that we often visit; a kind of limbo between astral planes. We all visit these spaces, but not everyone remembers them. When we do remember them, or lucidly know when we are there, we get the possibility to ascertain knowledge from those realms. Are the entities there real, just as real as the dream world itself? I often wonder if these beings we meet there are as Castaneda states, *inorganic beings*. He learns from Don Juan of the reality of inorganic beings and how they live and survive without metabolism or reproduction:

They are alive to the sorcerer/seer because they have awareness. This is the only criteria for life.

The inorganic beings thrive off of emotional states such as sadness, fear, dependency, and joy. For some sorcerers the inorganic beings become useful allies borrowing a person's energy to manifest semi-physical forms. For others they are draining and haunting nuisances. I wonder if the bird-woman is an inorganic I met in the dream world, if so, I feel she must be an ally.

The human dreamscape is vast indeed, and we should understand that man has been dreaming about higher living, as well as death, for eons. The ideas of a better way of life give us hope to survive the hard times we certainly endure. Dreams of death often translate into what our fears of the unknown are, and our unknown selves. Since we are self-conscious beings we have the knowledge of our present life and living state as well as our imminent death. Our fear of death becomes our nemesis and keeps the potential of living a life of liberation at bay. While our knowledge of death forces us to stay focused on the present moment, and do what is necessary to live; as we embrace death, as our greatest advisor, we learn the excellence of how to live. The ego consciousness is afraid of change, and the unknown, and so clings to the body and creature comforts.

We have been dreaming about death for so long we manifest our fears into the philosophies of the afterlife, or what comes after death. Philosophies are the intuitions of the collective consciousness. One such philosophy for a more primitive man revolves around burial rites. How must this primitive man have created understandings of dreams about death? He, over time, devised burial rites and death rituals, motions and actions to go through to remember their imminent end, for example, the names of Adam and Eve. The names are not historically proven to be attributed to actual humans who supposedly spawned the rest of humanity. The names are more iconic. The names have since been given to many people throughout the years, but originally had a significant meaning attributed to the angelic like quality man wants to remember about himself. The name Adam, in ancient Sumerian means "red earth" and the name eve means "plain of uncultivated land". Why?

Seven thousand years ago the Neolithic revolution occurred in the valley of Tibriz, which is present day Iraq. This is where the Garden of Eden was, according to biblical history. The Garden of Eden lies where the four major rivers crossed and forged, the Pishon, the Gishon, the Tigris, and the Euphrates. To the north and south of this crossing there are walls (mountains), and outside of these walls is the land of Nod. During this revolution death was common and feared. Life was hard and rituals were developed. Adam means red earth because the death rituals of the people of Eden used red ocher to paint the bones of the dead to offer them peace in the grave. They would wait until the buried body had decomposed, and dig up the bones and paint them red, and bury them again. Because we come into the world covered in blood, so shall we exit the world covered in blood, the blood of the red earth. Adam was thought of as the original man, this was to honor his name and the peoples that sprung forth from his loins.

All kinds of knowledge about ourselves and this life have been plucked from the dream world. It is an essential part of the human condition. We will continue to dream to access these worlds and manage our waking state with this sacred knowledge. There are many views of reality and we have to shake ourselves silly to realize whichever one we are currently in, is just a ripple on the surface of the infinite ocean of reality itself.

ThIrteen

THE HUMAN LINK TO SPIRIT

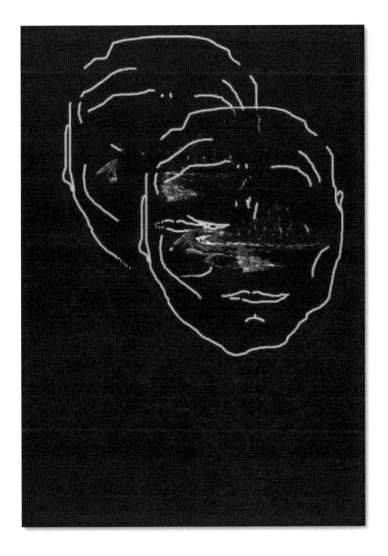

Back at Antoinette's house in La Jolla we were talking about working with the light. I always see the aura and light around and through her, every time I am with her. This event never ceases to amaze me; I talk to myself and say this is simply incredible. I actually peer into the spirit world every time I am with her. Truly I am in awe just contemplating it. I have this question I keep asking her; who is it, who is it, who is it that I keep seeing with the beard. After many times of my asking the same question she began to almost stop offering answers. She would be aloof and suggest that who it is, is really not important and I should not focus on the identity of the spirit. I still am eaten up by my own curiosity; I just feel that if I knew who it was I could glean some substantial information about myself in this whole process.

As time went on she seemed less interested in my quest and again told me the gift here is the light itself and that I am lucky enough to see it at all. My soul and spiritual state may not be attuned to the higher vibration to understand the intention of the God-force. She suggested I learn to meditate more often and more intensely, this will help me attune to the light. I know she is correct but I am impatient with myself, the world, and apparently the spirit too. So I study, read, contemplate and meditate for an answer. I did this for years until I just gave up. I just let myself be okay with never knowing who this blond bearded man is. I prayed for the answer and then stopped seeking it. I did resolve to the blessing that I am so very fortunate to have had this experience in my life at all and I just feel comforted by the whole thing. In my heart I know that this other reality, this other world, (and many more worlds for that matter,) is here in my consciousness. I know people would revel in this knowledge. I know that they are out there and also seek similar confirmation. For that I am eternally grateful. I believe that when I am on my death bed, I will remember and know this spirit world is right here awaiting me and my transition.

I also know others have similar confirmations in their lives. I've talked and read about people who have had a glimpse of the other side. I feel lucky to share this with them. The mystical wonderment of life is burned onto my soul with a bright light. Just like staring at the sun for too long and you look away only to still see the sun in your eyes;

this beacon of light that is Antoinette is with me wherever I turn to look.

Using my dislocated gaze I practice seeing auras from time to time. When I get out of the car at night, when I sit quietly with a morning cup of coffee, when surfing in the Pacific Ocean at sunset. For some reason the water combined with the mild exhaustion of surfing seems to bring about this phenomenon. I often see the subtle glow around my com padres when we surf together. It also seems to happen when the sun is not out, when it is overcast. It happens in the water many times when I don't even try to concentrate. I just look over at my buddy and he has a halo around him, it's so peaceful and calming to me; it lets me know there is abundantly more to this life.

Ever since this ability came to me I've tried to see the aura on myself in the mirror. Many times it has worked. I concentrate on a specific point on my face, and I focus on one eye, and dislocate my gaze, and slow my breathing. As my breathing slows, so does my heart rate, and then it becomes obvious that there is a correlation between the two. I can see the light fade in and out with my heart beat. The best view comes between breaths and as the breath gets more spaced apart, the clearer the vision becomes. I usually see a mild glow and mild color around my head. Plus the light comes out of the face itself, out of the features. The chin or brow, or the cheekbones will begin to glow. As I worked with this I have only seen one person appear; yes the blond bearded man.

As I stared at the luminous being I saw my own soul, myself in a band of vibratory consciousness, the move from matter back to spirit, the evolution of involution. There before me was a luminous being that I didn't recognize as a personality, but I knew it was intrinsically loving. It has taken me six years to see that it is myself coming through. The struggle to identify the being, or beings that I see, has become the journey through meditation of spirit regarding spirit. How it all works, I don't know. Maybe the being is an ally archetype, a psycho-physical manifestation of light. If the observer, and the observed, are one and the same; then what is the spirit manifestation before me? The light is not separable from me, we are one, and I perceive myself before me. I saw the blond bearded man clearly in the mirror, my face with more hair and a beard transposed on me. I stared and looked intently to see how much this picture resembled me. I looked older, more mature but still young and strong. I looked like a man, not a child. Could this really be me, looking at my older self? As time went on I realized that this figure was the only one I have ever seen in the mirror, and it's the only one ever transposed by me, so it must be a part of me, or linked to me. All the other beings I've seen with Antoinette were only seen with her, but this man was always seen with me in the mirror. I knew then whatever personality he is, is intimately mingled with myself, I've brought it home with me. I met my own self, my astral body, my double, my true self; the only problem is I don't know who he is.

On that day I learned another rule to the life code. This code of ethics, code of living, was beginning to develop, I knew I had to write it down and remember it. The new rule in the code is:

Our intent manifests our dream, the manifested dream materializes, but never as we actually envision it.

The link to spirit is an intrinsic part of being human, thus we call ourselves human beings. The breakdown of that word points to our ethereal side:

> *Hu* (breath) - *man* (mana, life)
> *being* (to be actively present)

equals the present breath of life. We as humans hold time/space from our top to our bottom; and from our front to our back. We are segments of time/space moving through time/space. Our very essence is ethereal and spiritual. Our spirit is linked to our bodily form, but our form is just a shell. We cannot afford to forget our soul nature. When we are active in the present moment, our ego consciousness is gone because we have no attachment to anything. Our state of being is tapped into the surrounding reality as well as the inner reality, and they are really polarities of the same thing. We then are linked directly with the universe, and conscious of it. Our link with intent is known and in the forefront of our mind. The longer we stay in this state the closer we get to spirit. The longer we stay out of this state the further we get from spirit, and the closer we get to the ego. Of course balance is paramount. When we fall, we get back up and decide again what it is we really should be intending.

It is odd that so many people don't see, or consider themselves as spiritual in nature. They decide that if they can't see, or touch, or measure something, then it has no validity. So they see themselves as only physical beings. Why then do our bodies produce heat, light, gas, sound, vibration? These all can be measured and seen! We generate energy constantly. Is that seen or measured? No, it is just known and accepted. We produce gases which again are not seen. We produce light and heat which are not seen by most people. These subtle qualities are known fact and yet are really in the realm of non-material aspects of us. If people can understand these subtle forms then why not the more subtle forms that dive deeper into the non-material?

It is only after ego death or transcendence of the mind that the highest stage of human existence begins, and that is the stage in which the body dissolves or yields to love and light. – Edward Plotki

Fourteen

STILL LEARNING

Adulthood is here and I stare off into space, a daydream where I contemplate without knowing it. When I snap back to the day or task at hand I become quiet. I am still learning. I went from a scared boy to an adult with fears. Each fear I identify I begin to conquer as I get to know it. I fell in love, I really loved. I loved another person with the intention of giving myself over to her, and always being willing to try to make happiness. I've loved many people in many ways. I let go, but I am still learning to let go. I let go of as much self destruction and self doubt as I am aware of. The self is amazing, a reservoir for whatever focused intent you fill it with, so I will not fill it with pity, doubt, or hateful emotion. The self is stunning in its creative power. For example, there is a foundation called the Long Now Foundation that has built a ten thousand year clock. It's completely mechanical. The time piece is designed to click on into the future for ten thousand years. It works with a series of weights and gravity. The purpose is to give people of today a different perspective on the present moment. So if you think our world today is advancing technologically now, then what do you imagine our world will be like in ten thousand years? If we can build a clock that can tick on for this long today, then what's next for tomorrow? In many ways our ancient ancestors attempted similar feats. Many civilizations recorded astronomic cycles of the stars that accurately map twenty six thousand year cycles that we modern humans use today. The clock stirs imaginations by those who see. One can't help but ponder the way things will be in ten thousand years. Amazing is the self of the human!

I am still learning, always. I've learned that we are intrinsically linked to God and spirit. I will not forget the fleeting glimpse I've seen. I've learned how tricky the ego can be, but I've learned how to stop the internal dialogue and transcend it. I am still learning.

FIfteen

CALVIN BROWN

When I was very small, maybe about five years old, I made my first true friend. It was my first true friend because I had no prejudice and no deceit within me. I was a whole human being. I assume everyone's first friend is a true one for these same reasons. My mother had a boyfriend named Randy, and he lived on a really big lake in Georgia. My mother and father were divorced when I was three years old. I only have a few childhood memories of them being together. My memories of my father from when they were still married are only memories of them as individuals. I remember the way my father looked with long hair, and a beard, and I remember him working out in the yard. I remember the tension and fear I felt when he caught me lying to him. He would squat down to my face level, and calmly look at me, and ask if I was lying, or telling the truth. He would look through me, and I knew even then that I couldn't get away with lying. I knew it bothered him. I could sense and feel my father's power when he looked at me and spoke to me. I had no choice but to respect him. So I never lied to him.

My mother's boyfriend had invited us over to the lake where I would walk down to the muddy shore, and spot tiny little frogs the size of a dime or a nickel. I'd find old turtle shells empty and muddied and throw rocks into the lake. Randy's good friend Calvin was over there at the house and we became friends instantly. Calvin Brown was an adult, and I don't know how old he was. We only hung out together a hand full of times, but we were pals from the start. I don't have very many memories of him or what we would do, but I remember his soul. For some reason I loved him. I suppose he loved me too, and I guess that's why we were such good pals. He was a smiling faced black man with a kind heart. I've been told these things about him as I grew older, but I remember his true and genuine personality as a child. I just chalk it up to a bond, a human connection. Maybe he never had a son, and so he took to me as his own, or maybe he just had a heart of gold.

I was so attached to Calvin that when we left the lake I always wanted to stay and hang out with him. So one day my mother let me go to Calvin's house, so that I could go dancing with his daughters. There were three of them, and I met them all, and as they were getting ready for the night, they said that I was going dancing with them. My mother knew the good man that Calvin was, and she trusted him to take good care of me since I was there to spend the night. I remember the girls all giving me lots of attention and hugging me and pinching my cheeks and such. I remember their house. The house was in the woods and not much more than a wooden shack. Built out of weathered gray and warped wood planks, it had a front porch about four feet high. The A-framed roof was tin, or some kind of rusted metal, and it had trees all around it. Georgia is a massive deciduous forest. The girls finally broke the news to me as they scurried out the door to go dancing, that I wasn't going. I was a little boy, and they were all young ladies. So they left in a big car as I watched the gravel driveway dust fly up.

It was dark and Calvin tucked me into bed, which was a cot in the main living room, the main room of the house. He left and I laid there in the dark. It was very dark out there in that forest. All I could see was a little moonlight shining through one of the windows across the room. I began to feel alone, and I got very scared. I just felt like I was the only one there and that everyone had left the house.

I don't know where Calvin was. I guess he was in the house somewhere, but I became more and more terrified as time passed. Then in the window that I could barely see, but could easily hear, was a buzzing wasp flying into the window. I could see the wasp between the window pane and the holey curtain. Smack, smack, in a rhythm it was flying into the glass. It just kept hitting the glass, and I got even more scared, and thought it would eventually come after me. I yelled, and cried, and cried some more, until Calvin came out to console me. He did, and he assured me that everything was fine, and stayed with me until I fell asleep.

It's funny how your imagination can be so powerful, and when you're a kid, some minor things seem so tremendously intense. I made it back to Randy's house the next day, and was glad to see mom again. I didn't ever go back to Calvin's house again, but we were still best friends. I suppose we hung out a few more times, and then he was gone. I remember mom sitting me down one day and telling me that my pal Calvin had died. It was the first time in my short life that I dealt with anyone dying; he was my best friend. All I remember was a heavy feeling of sadness that I would never see him again.

I still remember that feeling of loss, and missing old Calvin. I know as an adult that he and I had a bond, and a genuine friendship. He was a genuine type of person, and I am glad to have had such a friend. Maybe on some level our souls knew each other. Who knows, maybe we will meet again. I think about him and remember the view out of his window at night, moonlit curtains, and a terrible buzzing wasp. The view is still a vivid memory in my mind. I'll always remember my true friend Calvin Brown.

SIxteen

Tonal, Nagual, Toltec

Throughout my time wrestling with questions about God, the universe, and my human role in life, I found myself seriously seeking answers and truth. I assume that most anyone who is trying to find themselves will go through a similar quest, and learning curve. As I read, and study, and ask myself questions about the spiritual phenomena that I encountered, I found myself going back to the teachings of the Toltec's. I would like to say that I am by no means a spokesperson or authority on the subject, but I do feel a resonance and understanding with the subject. The Toltec to which I am referring is that of author and anthropologist Carlos Castaneda, who as far as I know, is responsible for bringing the subject to the modern western world.

I was first introduced to the Toltec teaching by my father, he had the first few books written by Castaneda. I would confide in my dad all the time seeking answers to my spiritual questions because he had shared with me some enlightening moments in his life. He and I always seemed to be open to the possibilities of the more subtle realms. He and I both have had our glimpses. So I would always ask him what my visions, and auras, and time with Antoinette all meant. He had good responses, but often left the answers up to me to decide. I will say we shared a lot. He never judged me or my lack of clarity. He was always caring and thoughtful with his assessment. We lived together for a short time in my early college years, and he treated me with respect, he treated me like a man. He would teach me lots of things that a young man should know when walking out in the world.

I remember him telling me about his creativity as a child; it being discouraged and stifled by his parents and adults in the family. He was a naturally creative boy with talent for music and drawing. He later became a stellar musician, writer, composer, and violin maker. His stifling childhood put a damper on his creative soul, and some emotional abuse may still be haunting him to this day. I feel unauthorized to say, I really don't know for sure. Still he has shared with me some encounters with the paranormal as well as psychic abilities. He is very intuitive, and can pick up on subtleties of character in most people. But his overly critical tool gets relied upon more than it should; I may have inherited this as well. It is much more convenient to pick apart someone else than to pick apart yourself.

100

Tide and the Crannog

He has told me of ghosts that he has seen and touched from time to time. They apparently have followed him to different homes and lingered for some years. He was terrified when they appeared because they were not really a bright presence, but more of an elusive and dark form. Over time he gained the courage to tell them to leave, or in some ways confront them. I think there were three different ones. He believed they were deceased family members, trying to tell him something. At a young age I was told this, so I grew up to some degree believing in the subtle realm; maybe this helped to open me up to it.

He also has seen auras and orbs and electro-magnetic fields in the desert. When I brought up my encounters with the light he was not shocked or surprised; and when I talked about auras he knew exactly how to describe them. I knew he had certainly been through similar events. It's hard to explain, but when I share this type of topic with people, I can tell whether they really understand, or not, by their reaction. The people who understand have at some level experienced the spirit world also. There is a kinship present. They don't look at me like I am crazy. I actually gave him the taping of my first session with Antoinette with the hopes of him listening to it and helping me sort through its meaning. To my disappointment, he lost it, and it will probably never be heard again. I did transcribe it before hand, luckily.

He and I would share books and topics; I grabbed his Castaneda books and went off to read them. It was a connection I understood immediately even though the writer uses a unique and self-created syntax. Castaneda's articulation of the spirit world and perception of reality were like music to my ears. Finally I felt like I now understood what I had been going through. His descriptions and use of mental tools accurately depicted some of my experiences. It made me feel like this was not only valid, but important and genuine. I knew that other people had been through similar mind-bending things as have I. After reading Castaneda's books many times I began to lean towards the Toltec way. I still see the similarities to eastern philosophy and others also, but the real life applications were just producing results. I ultimately find any form of practiced meditation will evolve one's consciousness, but each person has to choose the path that best resonates with them in their heart.

One of the many exercises that Castaneda talks about is the sweeping of the tonal. This is a mental and physiological move that I find works really well. Before attempting the move I should first briefly describe the tonal and the nagual. The tonal is one of the two aspects of the human mind/spirit. The tonal is attributed to right sided awareness while the nagual is the left. The tonal is what you are in right now, day to day, habitually carrying out tasks. It is upheld and constructed by our social conditioning and our internal dialogue. The internal dialogue is the inner voice you speak to yourself with everyday, all the time. The nagual is what is beyond all of that. The tonal is personal and small in comparison to the transpersonal and immense nagual. Both are intrinsic parts of the human being. Tonal is our self description, our habits, our beliefs, our emotional bodies, intellectual bodies, and physical bodies. It is the place where we spend most of our time. It is a place of constant duality, comfort and clinging. It needs to be swept clean in order to be transcended because it is an island, and the nagual is the never-ending sea.

Every day you spend time on the island of the tonal, it is all so common that you don't even realize that there is something more, out beyond what you know. When you sweep the tonal clean, on a regular basis, it becomes impeccably clean. This move takes time, but eventually you come to a place where there is nothing left to sweep, nothing left to clean. There you are on your tonal island and you have made it, you have made yourself impeccable. This process of focused attention is a meditation in itself; it brings you to focus on one thing and one thing only. Your focus becomes singular and clarity arrives. You are standing there on the tonal island, and then there is nothing left to do, but gaze out into the abyss, into the beyond. When you do, you begin to see the nagual out there. The infinite part of yourself, the part that you always knew you always knew, but never really acknowledged. When this occurs, a sense of freedom and expansion blankets you, and possibilities, and wonderment begin lapping up on the shores of the tonal, calling you unto your higher self. Pulling this maneuver off at will is the goal. It is a natural function for the human, but doing it does take quite a bit of personal power and focused energy. Sometimes it happens unknowingly; when in states of extreme fatigue or high stress, or at times of utter calm and relaxation. It is the natural process of evolution for the consciousness. The nagual is said to be the place where we find our individual truth. We find truth as it resonates to us personally. Things become clear and apparent, paths become illuminated, and decisions make themselves because you are seeing the energy of the universe as it actually is, as it flows through you.

Hearing the statement that "truth lies in-between" makes sense as the nagual is where we find our truth, and the nagual is said to be the space between all phenomena. When you tap into the higher state of the nagual, you relate to everything and your own self in new ways. You could say you know who you are. Still as you fade back to the monotony of the tonal to have layers of learning to peel away to know yourself again. Once learned the practice of leaving the island of the tonal, the process gives us a blueprint to follow in order to do it again. The blueprint is an energetic one as all these maneuvers require energy. It is ultimately a practice in meditation, but it is a practical one, one we can use every day. So imagine yourself on that island forever, and someday realizing you're stuck out in the middle of the ocean, alone. What do you do to create happiness and freedom? How do you leave the comfort of your little shore when all you see is never-ending oceans?

Our rationality often stands in our way. When I was first walking in the door to Antoinette's home I was skeptical of her clairvoyant abilities, but I have always been the kind of person who sensed and believed in something higher. Even as a child I believed in God. My parents never took me to church, or pushed any type of religion on me. At night my mother would teach us to pray to our guardian angels for peace and protection. I guess the prayers stuck with me. We often in our technological society rely on the rational to provide truth and value to our curiosities. This method is full of fallacy. There are so many aspects of the human, and his world, that cannot be tapped and measured with the rational mind. Those who disagree are just not thinking outside the box. In fact they are thinking too much, and feeling too little. When first introduced to the nagual we often become humbled, and then slowly realize that all our shortcomings, intellectual and otherwise, are the helpers along the way to expansion. Our shortcomings become milestones along the road to power.

My first introduction to the nagual was when I walked into Antoinette's door. I was split in two; one side had been completely living in the tonal, and now the other was opened up to the nagual. I must admit I've left my little island at times, but am by no means able to do it whenever I want. I have managed to do it at will, but still struggle with doing it consistently when I want. The point here is that

I was split in two, and I can never go back to unknowing the spirit exists, the nagual is here always.

As we travel the road to spirit there are many side streets and distractions along the way. They are intimately linked to our personality, personal history, self description, and short comings. All these distractions will eventually lead us back to the road to spirit. When you split in two the nagual always quietly beckons you to let go of the rational part of yourself to remind you that you are ultimately much more than the intellect or rational. The nagual beckons us all, just as death beckons us all, and will someday grab a hold.

Those who look at the surface of the sea must behold the birth and death of the waves, but those who seek the depths of the ocean behold one indivisible mass of water. – Yogananda

Until one is wholly under the influence of the independent wisdom of the soul, almost all that he is, and does, is a result of habit and conditioning. – Bagavad Gita v138

Ultimately we humans are destined to get better, destined to evolve, we just don't know it. Most of us feel the subtle connection to the spirit, God, or nagual. We just are too afraid to be still, and be with it. Ironically that is exactly what we really desire. All other desires are encompassed in the soul's desire to be reunited with spirit. It is such a shame that most modern religions have lost the very essence for their creation in the first place. So many men want to be powerful megalomaniacs and show the people around them that they have control, all the while never knowing what power is at all. It seems so simple to me; if you believe in a God, and you believe that God is love, then you can't justify killing another! No matter what scripture you ascribe to, if you're interpreting in such a way that you decide who lives and who dies, then you've misinterpreted the word of God. Every scripture (Bible, Toa, I Ching, Book of the Dead, Buddhism, Shinto, Kebra Nagast, Bahgavad Gita, Judaism, pagan scripture, Gnostic…) that I've ever read is designed to raise the consciousness of the reader. Every parable simply teaches a lesson about how to live a better life within yourself. Those who push their religions upon others, and cast judgment, are so egocentric they attempt to play the role of God. If you want to improve the world you live in, then start by improving yourself.

Master the restlessness that is synonymous with mortal life, and experience consciously the complete calmness or silence accompanying freedom from identification with the body. When such a devotee reaches this immutable state of perfection, he witnesses all the changes of life and death without being moved by them. Identification with the waves of changes leads to misery, or to live and find pleasure in the changeable is to be separated from the eternal. – Yogananda

Time went on, and I slowly began to form my own ideas about my paranormal experiences. I did intuitively come to some worthy conclusions. Still I have questions; still I have more to learn. I just keep working on trying to find truth within myself, find love within myself. I soaked up lots of religious theory finding over and over again the similarities of the messages. Most scripture is written for the purpose of reminding us about our good values, reminding us how to behave. Scripture is designed to uplift us. So I find that I cannot rely on one book, one bible, or one scripture alone. The Most High has too many names, and too many books, to be put into just one. I draw on many teachings to try to better my understanding of this life. I percolate another one of the nine ethics in the code:

Truth is a pathless land.
When facing many paths,
you must choose a path
with heart.

Seventeen

The Toltec Path to Freedom

Independent of which one enters, the ascents and descents of an impeccable spiritual journey will always lead one to that great stillness.
– Ed Mcgaa

All too often when scrutinized, organized religion falls short of uplifting those enrolled. Not unlike an academic institution, we find organized religion to be abiding by the same old teaching structures of the past. These methods are not producing very many saints, saviors, or enlightened people; on the contrary, they often produce a person who has no experience and only regurgitates what he was told. Why on earth would this suffice for a keen representation of a spiritualized person? Simply because that is what we've been taught. How many churches, mosques, or synagogues can you walk into across this nation and find a true spiritual giant? The truth is, holy people, enlightened people, are more likely to be found out in the street, or the park than in church.

The institution of religion has been a vital part of society for thousands of years, and during this time it has slowly become a vehicle for schooling and producing specific types of behavior which some societies consider advantageous. They are systematically producing individuals who think, feel, and emotionalize in basically the same way. The potential for controlling a population is much more effective if you curtail the way people think. If you haven't asked yourself, nor ever pondered these types of questions, then quite possibly you have been a product of such an organized religion. Today the power of multiple strains of media can influence an entire population into a few varieties of thinking patterns. The mainstream media is just like the cafeteria lunch line; you choose between a couple of food sources and that's what you eat. People eat what they are fed. The true facts about any event seen on television are scarce, and even unimportant to an industry that thrives on money and ratings. Like most people who thrive on money or ratings, the amount of validity and truth they produce is minimal. In some ways religion really is the opiate of society. That being said, it is a necessary one, it has brought us to where we are today. Today is the time for absolute freedom of thought. If you can't respectfully challenge your religion to its studied scholars without reprimand, then you should consider a more enlightened religion. All the ideas and thoughts are ultimately about a world unknown and rarely glimpsed, and still uncharted. Who can truly claim that they know and understand the essence of God? Yes, there are people who do experience the light of God, but still remain just an instrument for light to pass through. Most people just have to rely on the interpretation, and perception of those with experience, we trust them. But do they even really know?

If religion is condemning or killing other people, it is not truly acting out of love. It is also not allowing itself freedom.

In order for us to love, the creator has to have a form we can imagine, or at least feel; Although finite beings cannot know, until they have died, what an infinite being looks like". . – Fools Crow

Freedom is the liberating state at which souls begin to connect with spirit, it is natural and essential.

The un-manifested is spoken of as ever-existing, ever-conscious, ever-new bliss, in which the subjective spirit and it's perceptions of bliss are dissolved into one. . – Baghavad Gita v1.13

The devotee who realizes the personal God in a form will eventually realize him also in the omnipresent formless infinite.
– Baghavad Gita v15.34

I knew at an early age in Georgia, in a Baptist church, that I wasn't free. I could sense the dis-ingenuous intentions of the pastors, teachers, and adults as they looked at me and recited the rules. Even at eight years old, I knew to walk away from the unauthenticated behavior being acted out before me. I wanted to be myself, I wanted to be free.

The battlefield that lies beyond the description is the field of the unknown, the field where nothing is written down before hand; it is not the self or the world. It is the place where we can create, choose, or be anything we want to be It is the field of freedom.
– Castaneda

The description ofthe world, as I said before, is an agreement upheld as reality by our internal dialogue; and when we stop the internal dialogue we begin to see the reality drop away. With practice we can begin to move, and create, and manipulate the fibers of a new reality, hopefully with enough energy, one of total freedom. This maneuver takes years of practice and focused attention. The assemblage point is the point on our energy body, or luminous cocoon, where our reality assembles; and with practice we can move, and push this point to new locations on the luminous cocoon, creating and upholding an entirely new reality.

Don Juan warns Carlos that we forget that we have constructed the world we perceive through our commanding of the assemblage point to align the world as it does. Once the warrior learns to see, he can move his assemblage point from within. Having gained the sees that the world is created by the fixation of the assemblage point on the luminousbody of consciousness. The warrior who has lost the human form sees that nothing matters more than anything else. Never having been anywhere the warrior has no place to return. He reassembles the world through his exercise of controlled folly, and lives out his life with total awareness in total freedom. . – Castaneda

The warrior on the path of knowledge and self discovery teaches us a fundamental lesson, I remember it and incorporate it as my own, as part of the code.

Anything can be accomplished with focused energy!

Eighteen

Family and Friends

As I lay in the hospital, my bed in an uncomfortable position, with wires and tubes crossing my lap, I realized what I already know, but reaffirm; the people you keep in your life are extremely important and instrumental to your personal growth. I think we all know this but sometimes need to be reminded. As Machiavelli teaches us; you will be judged first by the company you keep. They are a decent barometer, telling others of your morals and values. I am in the bed and just watching television as a small group of friends just left my bedside, I am alone again. These people took the time out of their busy day and busy lives to come to see me in my time of depressed illness. They all saw me at a vulnerable and unpleasant state. I am basically not the alpha male I portray myself to be. They get to gaze upon my helpless, meekness, struggling to be positive.

The silver lining here is that I get to find out who among my social group really cares about me. This is such a valuable lesson because the actions of people are what really shine through in who people are. As they all left and went back to their busy lives I am uplifted by the simple feeling that people care about me, and may even love me. They all gesture in their own unique way, bring gifts and food, and things they know will give me hope. It is priceless, it is heartfelt, and it is what a friendship is all about. It is also a giant contrast to the feeling I had when I accepted that the woman there beside me, didn't want to be there.

Not much of my family could actually be there in the hospital with me, because they all live hours or days away, but they all called, and made contact to show their love and support. Again, being loved and respected by those closest to you is unbelievably valuable. It makes you confident that you also know how to love and be friends, how to give and receive. As self-aware beings we need to know such things to evolve and feel whole. I know if I was truly alone, with no friends or family caring for me, I would recover much more slowly. I thank all those bright people who make their presence known, to help another in need, without you, I would be lost. Death is our greatest advisor; and when facing the possibility of dying, we become more aware of our purpose and desire. Just the idea that our death is coming for us someday causes us to live life more fully. I just want those friends and family members to know how well loved they are. I know that most friends in life come and go, and very few last for a long time, but still when they are there, and genuinely care, it is crucial for the spiritual camaraderie.

To the ancestors and grandparents who blazed the path of life before us, and to those who walk in the spirit world now, looking over us, I give my love, respect, and gratitude. I've had many friends in my life, traveled to foreign lands, relying on their trust and companionship for growth. I will do my best to uphold the core values that keep this bond alive by not being too selfish, and by being willing to lend a hand when needed. Our social family is valuable and instrumental in keeping us on the good path.

True friends are precious, rare, and hard to find. If you have one, keep them close to your heart.

Nineteen

RIVER HEAD

Time keeps passing, I still wonder who and what I've seen in the light. The spirit realm lets us know, now and then, that we are connected. I wonder why we can't understand better this connection, why is it so mysterious? What is the meaning of all this? As soon as I find some substantial meaning to the river flowing through my head, it turns on itself and changes. I grasp a "sensical" direction and feel accomplished; then, it undulates into something that now needs my search for meaning. Again I grasp for meaning. I guess to some extent meaning itself is a paradox. We are conditioned to seek it and affirm it's all encompassing power, its finality. But as we already know, as far as we can tell, all of this…..is infinite, so where is the final meaning in that?

There is an intuitive part of me that grasps the meaning of no meaning, the religion of no religion, the doing of not doing; the Zen of things. Indeed it is a very hard concept to describe. It's more like a description of the indescribable. So where am I? Where are we? How does one make sense of it all? Bust open the river head and let it flow as freely as possible and understand that at any moment in life your core self will change, forever, in the blink of an eye!

I am still on the quest to rationalize and determine my experience; in some ways, that is what this book is about. Since I receive no concrete answers from the glowing beings I see in the light, and since they reoccur, I seek the expertise of others with similar experience to help define my reasoning. I won't pretend that my assessment is correct; it is merely my best attempt so far. I am still learning.

The blonde bearded man I keep seeing in the light, and in the mirror, is somehow important to me. He reveals himself as if his stare is transmitting knowledge. Although I can't say what this potential knowledge is, still I do feel a powerful presence when he shows. As best I can ascertain he is a reflection of myself, and is reveling my deeper self to my conscious self, introducing them so as to expand. This is sort of like the principle idea of the dreamer seeing himself in the dream. The dreamer is meeting his dreaming body, which allows the dreamer to wield new and intending power in the dream; but more importantly, new intending power in the dreamer, himself, in both the dream world and the waking world. It's an overall process of expansion. So I may be actually meeting myself to expand myself. This is not that far-fetched, we do it all the time; our own inner voice talks to us, reminds us, remembers to remember and such. Think about prayer, who is listening to your prayer, who grants the prayers fruition? Is it God? Is it nature? Is it you? Humans are by nature self conscious, aware of your own self. Meeting myself reflection in the ethereal world could be my consciousness being self-conscious.

It's completely common for ourselves to reveal ourselves to ourselves. In times of critical situations people report all kinds of extraordinary things they witness. I was once sliding off the road in a sharp curve while driving in the rain. The crash probably took no more than 4 seconds, but I made decisions to steer, lift my foot off the gas, let go of the wheel, and cover my face while spinning at sixty miles an hour. All this was going on and I could see the car from above it. I had a floating view of the crash as it was happening. Somehow my "self" was protecting itself by being aware of itself in a critical situation. We uncover ourselves by ourselves constantly.

The man I see may be, as I believe him to be, *the mold of man*. This term is from Carlos Castaneda in his book *the **Fire From Within***. His explanation of his experiences is the one that resonates with me the most; I am comfortable as of now, with it. As I understand it, Castaneda learns from Don Juan that the mold of man is the universe's way of stamping man with a certain state or condition; it is what defines the difference between humans and other species. The mold of man is just as it sounds, a mold, or a die that stamps our humanness on a blob of conscience/energy. He also says that all species have a mold unique to them, however humans have the capability to witness their own mold, and most other creatures do not. For someone on the path of knowledge, seeing the mold of man is critical to attaining knowledge, moreover, once you see it, it changes the world as you know it. Even more important, at some point the next step is to see it on your own, unaided by a guide, teacher, or sorcerer. The main reason to pull off this maneuver is because most people who witness it succumb to defining it as God himself. He said:

To see it on my own, unaided by anyone, was an important step because all of us have certain ideas that must be broken before we are free; the seer who travels into the unknown to see the unknowable must be in an impeccable state of being.

116

Tide and the Crannog

Our rational assumptions and our fears prevent us from being free and impeccable; they hold us back from freeing up enough energy to see the mold of man, as well as understand what it is. The freeing up of energy cultivates our personal power and gives us the freedom to be what we want, and be free.

Old seers, as well as mystics of our world have one thing in common - they have been able to see the mold of man, but not understand what it is. Mystics throughout the centuries have given us moving accounts of their experiences, but these accounts, however beautiful, are flawed by the gross and despairing mistake of believing the mold of man to be an omnipotent, omniscient creator; and so is the interpretation of the old seers, who call the mold of man a friendly spirit, a protector of man.

With this interpretation one becomes confronted with the age old question of God's existence, I am not in any way challenging this. The point here is to rethink our relationship to the Almighty, for oneself, and not rely on the easy regurgitation of the local corner church whose typical goal is to fill the tithing or donation box. Like most spiritual matters, God is a personal one, existing within the self, not the church. A faith is at best a second-hand account of belief. Without direct experience, contact, or seeing, most people form a belief that really has no validity at all. Even still, Castaneda learns that if one is able to see the mold of man he almost certainly submits to the same mistake of the modern mystic, and is over-whelmed by the vision, and automatically assumes that it is God. The presence is incredible, the light shining around, and on you, gives you the feeling of harmony, love, peace, warmth, and that you are truly loved. Everything is in its right place, and you are blessed by the sight. It is a true mystical experience that moves the assemblage point of reality. For me, I think it is a step into knowledge that you cannot go back from, only forward to. The desire to bow down and subjugate yourself in ultimate gratitude is overwhelming. It is also my understanding that the spirit guide/ nagual is responsible by their sheer power for catalyzing the vision. I sincerely doubt that it would ever have occurred in my life without the aid of Antoinette. Although I have witnessed the spirit realm away from her presence, the doors of perception swung open the day I met her.

As I gazed into the light with all the passion I was capable of, the light seemed to condense and I saw a man. A shiny man that exuded charisma, love, understanding, sincerity, truth. A man that was the sum total of all that was good. The fervor I felt upon seeing that man was well beyond anything I had ever felt in my life. I did fall on my knees. I wanted to worship God personified, but Don Juan intervened and whacked me on my left upper chest, close to my clavicle, and I lost sight of God. — Castaneda

For me, the incomprehensible God has now been witnessed in daylight and sobriety, but the image before me is a blonde-bearded man, who actually looks a lot like me. So as Castaneda further discovers, the mold of man falls short of God himself mostly because of the personification; meaning the image of God cannot possibly be a man, a male. This is because something so incomprehensible to us is rendered in terms/forms that are familiar to us. The God-force may be in fact behind manifestations that mystics witness, but they see in terms of their own human limitations. So God is seen as a man by most men and as woman by most women. This is the mold of man, seen; the die that stamps us as human.

I think many such occurrences happen throughout the world, when a soul is ready and responsive to knowledge. People see the mold of man as shiny glowing beings or as a light, the light of the God-force. It creates an undying love and loyalty to the spirit, and I continue to think that my blonde-bearded man is somehow here to expand who I am, teach me to grow, and reveal myself to myself at deeper and deeper depths. I take comfort in my assumption. Only time will uncover my undulations of understanding.

Gods come and go, they live and die, but the mold of man survives. The mold of man is an intrinsic part of the species itself. The mold of man survives and thus God survives.

Twenty

Pain and Change

My ability to consistently move doubt is at the moment, dwindling. I admit I am weak and fragile. It's not something I reveal easily. With all the spiritual lessons I've learned and believe I've applied, I still find the struggle with intense bodily pain is often defeating. I know that to achieve success in life one must consistently move doubt, but for some reason the pain in my lower back has resurfaced yet again, and doubt is hovering over me like a storm cloud.

I wrote earlier that this issue had been healed, and yet something in my body remained unsettled. The former turns out to be wrong and the latter correct. What is this pain doing here again? It has become my nemesis, my agony. The nerves running along my spine are constantly impinged and thus draining my daily energy to be the man I want to be. It is so frustrating to live this way, and for those who have never had serious back issues, you are very fortunate, and simply cannot understand.

This is the sobbing in my heart, it's the heaviness of my life; it's what makes the ups so high, and surely the lows so very low. For me it's almost unbearable. The pain is so intense and debilitating, I can just barely move. Each little task becomes huge. I feel that the level of tension and frustration could bring on the loss of want, desire, and sanity for living. I cry. As I am writing, I cry. I, again find myself on the floor thirteen years later, facing the same problem. I lie on the floor and use a foam roller to stretch and decompress my spine. I assume I use this tool more than the average person. I do get relief, and the stretching for me is more about the myofascia and nerves along the spine, and not so much the muscles. At times I will lie on this foam tube for up to an hour just focusing on a fingertip size spot, which still will not let go. I've had tension in this particular spot for thirteen years or so. Now this spot is causing serious pain. All the other tightness is related to this spot and seems to respond in kind, but the one spot is lifeless and still stagnant.

I find myself mentally exhausted, fighting against the pain for the last six weeks. I am on the floor, and for the second time in my life, I am openly accepting the prospect of death. This time I am considering taking my own life. I am so tired of being in pain; I am so tired of having that pain rob me of the things that make me happy. I am on the floor with tears of pain and melancholy. I am thinking of the people I love and will leave behind, they won't understand. If I leave this world in suicide they won't respect what life I've lived. At this point they are what keep me here on this concrete floor.

For me, life is not worth living if I can't make myself and others happy. If I can't do the things I love, and I can't be a complete person, living is not that great. If I can't be a man for the women I love, or a father to my unborn children, if I can't make my beautiful curly haired woman happy, then life is without purpose. I know suicide is irresponsible, and in some ways the easy way out, but relentless pain is cause for me to strongly consider a way out. As long as pain is changing, then it is manageable. When pain is constant and unchanged, it becomes fragmenting and lethal. If my life continues with this level of debilitation and pain, I just will check out…disappear.

I stand up, it takes me some time. I look in a sliding glass door as a mirror. My spine is noticeably crooked; I am half a man at best. I cry again and think about the faces of the people I love. I've found the woman I think I will marry; I truly love her tenderness and sweet demeanor. I would hate to hurt her; I know her heart will be crushed. I want her with me now, but I can't stand to appear so weak in front of her. I am tormented by the pain. My family, how will they cope with my absence, will they forgive me? They made me who I am; I am a part of them. Parents are not supposed to deal with such loss. Do they know I love them and respect who they are? I hope they don't judge me. I hope they could understand how painful life has become for me. So many thoughts go through my mind, so many faces of people I love, it's all so mind-bending. I simply want relief. I don't know if I'll get it on the other side. I hope the pain stops. I have goals and dreams that I once thought I could achieve, but the pain is so intense, it's foreboding.

On the phone, the next day, I am talking to my brother, Ian. Actually I spent most of the time complaining about my pain and lack of hope. I was at a standstill, seriously doing nothing, just moping in my pain. Ian suggested I contact an old friend who treated me with acupuncture years before. I dismissed the idea and stated that I didn't know how to contact him; I had lost his phone number. He suggested that I simply search his name on Google. I brushed it off. I decided to try it the next day and voila, he came right up first on the list; Mr. Gregory Lipton, L.Ac. I e-mailed him; he sent his number back and asked how I was doing. Soon we spoke on the phone, and briefly caught up. I went to see him at his practice the following day. Greg looked the same, still fit and in good spirits. His kind, wise eyes and tough brow looked at me surveying my state of health. He listened to my painful story and began the acu-puncture treatment. I laid down on a table, and he pin-pointed certain sensitive pain points along my spine and hip and shoulder. We talked more while he put a series of needles in. I could immediately feel the connection between some points creating pathways along my body. I remember this sensation from ten years earlier; the electrical pulses and warm relaxing muscles. He did some adjusting to the needles and rolled over a heat lamp for my lower back.

There are a couple spots of extreme tension along my neck, I said to him. He prodded and placed a few needles near where my neck meets my shoulders. It felt better, dull, achy, and better.

He left me there for a while to relax and let the treatment set in. Soothing Asian music plays softly in the room, I relax. A strange tension in the back of my neck began to come on. It felt like a tight bang wrapped around the base of my neck. I could almost sense a low humming tone in my ears. I let it hum and slowly move about. The tightness moved around to the front of my neck but inside my body. I felt a flow of electricity or energy in the middle of my throat, it was an odd feeling. It continued and slowly the tension on the back of my neck let go, and my throat was flowing with chi. A little time went by, and the throat relaxed and seemed to open near where my thyroid might be. The whole event reminded me of a year earlier when I had plum pit chi (a painful build up of toxins that localizes in the throat) from having typhoid fever. I may never know, but intuitively I linked a connection between the two events. I had a severe lump/migraine headache in my throat for five months; my pain body remembers what it was like.

After all this time, I thought I was over the plum pit chi, but only when the release during this acupuncture session occurred, do I think it really ended. I hope so. The release sent a warm and relaxing sensation through the neck, shoulders, and back. It was an energy flow that brought some balance to the tension in my upper body. It was an amazing event that sunk my neck into the table for relief. All this manifested by a couple of hair-sized needles at the hands of a great healer and friend, Gregory Lipton, L.Ac.

If fear stops us from manifesting our destiny, then what am I afraid of? What fear could possibly be causing such dysfunction in the body? I have run out of possible answers, I don't know. I am beginning again to not fear death, I may be welcoming it.

A week passes, I show signs of improvement. My back is getting better and the muscles around the spine seem to be relaxing a bit, this gives me hope. When another full week goes by, and even with the improvement, I still can't bring myself to go to work, I just still feel the sensitive spot on my spine, it is not healing fast enough for me. I thought I'd be making some money by now, but it's been 20 days of recovery and the pain is still there. Greg Lipton treats me with needles and every session brings about progress, but I am now faced with the real possibility of financial ruin, and losing much of what is dear to me. The swinging back and forth between possibility and hopelessness is as fragile as the twinge of nerve pain from a hard sneeze. Things are so temperamental, my future really changes with the wrong sneeze. What kind of future is this?

I ponder how I will sell all my stuff, and move back in with my parents. The loss would be gigantic. If I can't get back to work soon, my bills will be in delinquency, my credit shot, and my potential for a better job and a happy relationship squandered. I try to think of something else but the worry is too great. I am frightened to lose the woman I love to such a trivial thing, a compressed disc in my spine. How would I tell her why I must leave her? I, like a child, would live 2,640 miles away from her because I need my mommy; how depressing. I always thought of myself as a strong man, a capable man. I've been successful in most endeavors, but this is the worst way to lose at love. I just ache at the thought of being without her, and I cringe at the idea of not being able to fulfill her. It's just a slipped disc, or pinched nerves; it's a ball of toil, a world of pain.

The idea of losing everything is terrifying, unless you've got nothing to lose. I just don't have the Zen state of detachment in this situation; I have too much to lose.

Sitting around in pain, with no money, and bills piling up; eating cereal for breakfast, lunch, and dinner; it all just sucks. I try to heal myself. I look into the psyche and face my emotional pain. I'll do most anything to get healthy. Could my history of back pain be linked to my childhood? I remember lots of pain and frustration as a child. When will it end, when will I transcend it? From a very early age I was the receptacle for pushes, punches, and hold-downs. My older brother and I deposited our anger and resentment on one another daily. Being attacked tormented me, and I always took it the best I could. I tried to be strong, and I was, but I know it shaped my personality in some ways. My inner child felt mostly confusion. Why was he hitting me again, and why so often? I asked myself over and over…why? What did I do to warrant such attacks? Sometimes it was very bad. Frustration was as common in my childhood, as it is now in my adulthood. I grew older and frustration became resentment and anger. Anger can make you unhealthy. It made me feel unwanted by him, my brother. In my adult life, he and I are the best of friends, and we love each other genuinely. He has been there for me always, without question, and I don't blame him at all for my current state. I simply want to purge myself of any emotional hindrance I may have in my inner child. I want to forgive myself for harboring such anger and frustration. It does me no good now, I let go.

I have no regrets and I know I am a summation of my personal experience. All my past is what I am in the present moment and they define one another. Each aspect mutually creates the other. There is a Zen Koan that says:

The tree shows the bodily form of the wind; waves give vital energy to the moon. The mind creates the self as much as the self creates the mind. We lose this truth when we are grasping at life. I have no other self than the totality of things of which I am aware. – Alan Watts

The next ethic in the code of ethics for me bubbles up:

Self pity and self importance are a waste of energy and lead to self destruction.

I have to admit though, that I am grasping at life, I am seeking freedom from pain.

Zen is whatever you are doing now, not what you are seeking – Alan Watts

Right now I am seeking.

Twenty – One

The Faster You Pursue Your Shadow, The Faster It Flees

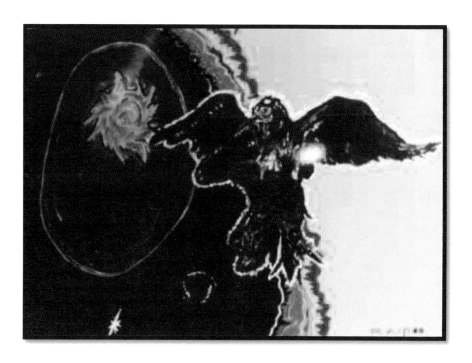

The burden of enlightenment is, well, to me, **unknown**. I have no firm idea of what enlightenment is. Possibly it is the accumulation of random epiphanies throughout life. The Buddha's do, however intrigue me with their koans and approach. If I understand it correctly, the process of figuring out a koan can stimulate epiphany, and the epiphany is the answer. But the point is not to archive the answer; it's to engage in the process. The process is closer to enlightenment. So just like that, smack, enlightenment just happens.

up in the middle of the x, knowing it will fall easily by morning. I walk back to the house and feast.

The decompression of the short holiday was much needed and a lot of fun. I remembered my need for happiness. I remembered the things that make me happy; Loving friends, loving family, the love of my beautiful curly haired girlfriend, her fingers through my hair, being in nature, riding waves, the hum my motorcycle, the sound of uilleann pipes over the sea, and being able to ponder one wondrous thought at a time.

I left the next evening at dusk. I hugged my brother and father good-bye. I drove down the dusty driveway and then reversed the car. I backed up over the the little six lined drawing I had made. The stick had fallen over in the east/west direction. I was on the road again heading toward the setting sun, where things dissolve; I was chasing that which disappears. I was feeling fine. Like that little stick, I was pointing west.

Anger. Sometimes you want to destroy something. Sometimes you want to pull out your hair. Mankind is afraid, as I am afraid. That is why religion is born. Religion is a way to behave so as to keep our fears away, or at bay. The word (religion) means to tie to or bind; so we bind ourselves to systems to keep out the fear. Still we are afraid. I made my little drawing in the sand, my little ritual for direction to keep me moving away from fear. I am in essence bobbing in the ocean of time. I don't think there is really an end, only change. That cactus told me we are always between our eternal self and the constant washing away of who we are. We are always ebb and flow, always. Years ago, my dad and I were talking about the nature of spirit. I probed him for answers to religious questions. My dad was correct years ago; he said the answer to "it all" is "there is no answer".

We are no less a Buddha asleep than when awake. So to save life, life must be destroyed, and one word settles heaven. And when I am full of anger I am just a fool.

Twenty-Three

Keeping the Island Alive

Love walks into your life, and just as fast it vanishes. You wake up one day and it's gone from your heart. Just like you wake up one day and a pudgy little role of fat appears around your waste line. It wasn't there yesterday, but voila, it is there today. Love is such a tricky thing. It is even tricky to talk about. All I know is that it is essential for life, essential for a healthy life, essential for a graceful death, and keeps us awake by slapping us open-handedly over and over and over. Love, like God, is the great teacher.

We all secretly yearn for love from someone. It's this yearning, like challenges, that pushes us on to keep trying in life. Battles in life bring us to the center of ourselves. I am looking through darkness. I must be focused to succeed, it's the only way to be in the darkness, but shining my own light, the light given to the human evolution, the soul is the light. I keep trying for something more, something better, to become something new. My battles are elegantly designed to hone the ability to burn from within, to be my own light. Heartache is just part of the package; we all have to have it. At some point in your life you will love, and at some point you will lose that love. You will feel the hard slap of love. Most likely, this will repeat itself many times throughout your life. Love is like the sunlight; just about everything is desperately searching for it. The planet's species compete for it so vigorously; they will strangle their neighbors for it. There are some biological species deep in caves, and in oceans that survives completely without sunlight, like the crystal formations in the lechuguilla cave in New Mexico. I wonder if there are people out there who can live without love. It feeds everything, then kills the old, and the weak, and feeds itself on their old bodies; reincarnating and recycling their energy to make more love to go

140

around. Love is deadly, and we all desperately need it.

That being said, I am not an expert on love, I am just the one slapped around by it, willing and waiting for the next open hand.

To keep the island healthy and prosperous, we have to constantly look after it; we have to learn to love. To keep it growing in awareness we have to sweep it and maintain cleanliness. To keep it alive we have to find love, and to find love we have to use whatever talent we've got, and create love. Love begets love. Tapping the inner source of who we are, and creating love from within, is not as easy as it sounds. Our fears and selfishness hold us back. No man is an island, but we have to keep our island alive. No man is an island, but in some way all men are alone, like an island. An island can be right next to another island, but it is still alone as it's own island. So to accomplish a bounty of love we have to learn to put aside our indifference, and act on the heart's intelligence.

Intelligence is rightly guided only after the mind has acknowledged the inescapably of spiritual law.
– Swami Sri Yukteswar

A crannog is an ancient Celtic island. It is man-made and usually in a lake or river. The crannog is often round and has walls surrounding it. During times of war and trouble the ancient Celts would go to these islands for the purpose of defending themselves. Only accessible by boat, they could always see their enemies coming, giving them the advantage of preparation in battle. No man is an island, but we are all man-made crannogs, preparing for battle each day.

Consciousness must always remain the smaller circle within the greater circle of the unconscious, an island surrounded by the sea. Within the ocean of unconsciousness he perceived an endless and self-replenishing abundance of living creatures, a wealth beyond our fathoming. – Carl Jung

So, alone we are born into this world and alone we exit into the next. Yet we get and give energy to our kinship. We are social creatures. For this reason, we get and give energy. We are an island alone, being bombarded by the changing tides. We evolve by the force of our death that is always pursuing us; it is a sharp and refined existence. This is why for the Yaqui Indians death is our greatest advisor. It is relentlessly stalking us and the next ethic in the code is that

Death is our greatest advisor.

Death teaches how to learn and what is really important to learn. Death teaches us the true value of life. Learning these things is another endeavor all together. We need a teacher, like Antoinette, someone who has knowledge to pass on. Then we can access the realm of spirit called the nagual:

> *When a sorcerer is dealing with the nagual he must give the instruction which is to show the mystery to the warrior. And that's all he has to do. The warrior who receives the mysteries must claim knowledge as power by doing what he has been shown.* – Castaneda

It is of the human condition to sway between the tonal and the nagual, but the nagual is always there for us to access, as we realize the need to know ourselves. Most times we operate in the tonal where we are habitual and hold on to our self-descriptions, where we grasp and cling to emotions, intellect, and comforts. This is the place of duality. The process of sweeping the island/crannog/tonal gives us an energetic imprint. The sweeping and cleaning of the island helps us remember who we truly are. It is ultimately a meditation reconnecting us to the nagual. It is within the individual experience of the nagual that we find truth. The more we do it, the better we get, it is cumulative and energizing.

142

Tide and the Crannog

Without struggle in my life, and without pain and discomfort, I would probably never have had the urge to become more self aware. Like many people, this urge doesn't occur until doom, or catastrophe rattles the gate. So, I would never have written such things. I would probably never have met the lovely Antoinette. The awakening mind is innate in us, but must be coaxed out by direct experience of the nagual, our link to spirit. It's my best guess that it is full of both pleasure and pain.

It's raining; the storm is on the horizon. I am staring it directly in the face. I am my crannog! The rain seeps into the soil around the shore and the tidal surges pull the soil into the sea. Tiny grains of my crannog are being eroded from me constantly. The tide is relentless, it won't give up, it thrashes my shoreline everyday; changing the coast one wave at a time. At any moment the core self will change anew, I can wait for it to happen, but cannot expect it. The action of expecting it is a projection into the future, which of course is always in front of us. I keep the island alive; I sweep it with Zen-like diligence. The knowledge of my impending death peeks at me from around corners from time to time; reminding me of its pursuit. Before it catches me, I pray that I will have acquired the love in life to peacefully embrace it when the time comes. The time we spend in bliss, meditation, is the nagual's preparation of the heart to transcend the transgressions of the little self, the ego. Imagining the poise and presence it must take to face death with a loving heart, is barely within the grasp of the mind, just barely. The warrior on the path of knowledge lives his life just for the potential of this moment. Let go!

Do you think that the world you have known all your life is going to leave you peacefully, without any fuss or muss? No! It will wriggle underneath you, and hit you with its tail. – Castaneda

Every time I think of my sessions with Antoinette I am still boggled by the other realm. I have shared the generalities with a few people close to me; they almost can't react in earnest. I sense them trying, but I see the disconnection brought on by the inability to relate. They just have never experienced such a thing. The writing here, itself, may be just the same for most people, just another description of the world. I genuinely hope not, but must accept the possibility. The other realm, the nagual, is infinite to the Yaqui, and the Yaqui sorcerer's goal is to go there at will, and be conscious of it.

I was nineteen when I first saw the light, the energy of the universe. At that age it overwhelmed me and I still have not recovered. I put a very dear friend of mine, Teresa, a sassy British woman, in touch with Antoinette. She waited months to see her, and she called me when she finally did. Teresa's experience in the light was remarkably similar to mine. She peered at the glowing great masters shining through Antoinette. The room filled with light and wrapped around her. I feel blessed to have facilitated the meeting in her life; such an experience is so profound and rare. Teresa was amazed just like me, but because she was a grown woman at the time, she spoke about it with perspective and ease; something I still can't do. I believe with time the experience will mark a keystone moment in her life. She is such a good-hearted woman. This also bonds us as friends who have shared the witnessing of the light; a remarkable experience.

For Don Juan this event was what made humans into sorcerers –

He stated that what made human beings into sorcerers was their capacity to perceive energy directly as it flows in the universe and that when sorcerers perceive a human being in this fashion, they see a luminous ball, or a luminous egg-shaped figure. His contention was that not only are human beings capable of seeing energy directly, as it flows in the universe, but that they actually do see it, although they are not deliberately conscious of seeing it. – Castaneda

Tide and the Crannog

Witnessing the light-energy, as I said, changed who I am, it shifted my perception of reality instantly.

Don Juan went on explaining that the moment one crosses a particular threshold in infinity, either deliberately, or, as in my case, unwittingly, everything that happens to one from then on is no longer exclusively in one's own domain, but enters into the realm of infinity..........The actions of sorcerers are exclusively in the realm of the abstract, the impersonal. Sorcerers struggle to reach a goal that has nothing to do with the quests of an average man. Sorcerers' aspirations are to reach infinity, and to be conscious of it. – Castaneda

Being conscious of infinity opens the door for intent to enter the equation:

The active side of infinity is one's intent,
The active side of infinity is one's intent;
The active side of infinity is one's intent!

So what is the intent in one's life, in one's death, in one's heart, on one's crannog? The answer to this question is paramount. The intent of my desire, or the intent of my quest, is so ambiguous. Boiling it down, my thoughts and desires, my life's purpose; what do I want? Really, how does one decide on one's life intent? I toil, and my mind squirms. How are true answers going to come to me about such abstract yet paramount concepts?

I know the core of being holds a sacred knowledge which can reveal the answers if unlocked, if accessed. At the center of us all, is the link to intent, our access to the infinite! Have you ever been rattled at your core? I ask myself more than once. Seeing beyond this ordinary realm creates little trembles that vibrate out of your soul and ring a teaching when they hit together at a certain frequency.

I stood looking in the eyes of a no-named belligerent drunk demanding I fight him. Survival mode takes over; I prepare at all cost to defend myself. His liquid courage is a front hiding some childhood insecurity; however its anger is aimed at me. I prepare to kill if need be, it's a realistic option, although not one I wish to choose. Sober, I can see the weakness in his lying eyes; his anger is not truly for me. He pities himself and doesn't want to admit it. His reality is a constant escape from sobriety, he's angry with himself because he knows he is inauthentic. I take a stand because he threatened me; I was just in the wrong place at the wrong time. My stand is real. It is to defend myself at all cost, but to not hurt anyone. I've bloodied a person before; I know how bad I felt the next day knowing I truly hurt someone. His anger charges mine, he knows now if he really commits he'd better be sure he can defend himself, and well. We managed to never hit each other, a good thing for us both, but the primordial animal has risen within me, remembering the animal part of my core. One quick punch to his throat and he's permanently injured, I could see the fear in him, I could see that he could see his mistake. I could see through him.

With those wet winds lashing, and a constant tide on all sides, my crannog needs defending. It requires its own intent. Floating on the sea, ever-changing and natural, even my own nature attempting to destroy me; I see lightning and hear thunder. At once, the onslaught, the whipping rain and clashing thunder goes silent. A time warp, a bend in space, silence is present among the tempest. I begin to remember peace. Everything slows and perspective changes.

Inner silence is the stand from which everything stems in sorcery, in other words everything we do leads to that stand, which like everything else in the world of sorcerers doesn't reveal itself unless something gigantic shakes us. – Castaneda

Tide and the Crannog

    My island is alive, living and pulsing. The wonderment and mystery of the world, and beyond, rattles me, and all in one moment I am empty; an empty cage. Submerged in inner silence, I feel the boundaries lifted off in expansion, into infinity. My intent unknown, blurs are becoming clearer, I know we all want to love someone, something. My crannog is adrift and alone, white-knuckled against the ocean.

Special thanks to:

Teresa and **John Rundle,** for the editing process, listening intently, and opening your hearts as a neighbor. You are as always great friends.

Erin Wertman, for the writing process, editing insights, and help along the way.

Evan Smith, for helping and directing the photography.

Ian McMahon, for your endless support and friendship in this world. Thank you for being an active part in this publication and for the foreword and my deepest friend.

Bob James, for encouraging me in this process, editing and keen insight, believing in me. You are a beautiful soul!

Mary James, For just about everything else. Your love, support, and belief in me is the foundation of my success. I thank you endlessly for your loving wisdom and there is no way I could have done it without you.

Antoinette Spurrier, for your blessing for me to share our experience publicly. For opening the realm of light to me and touching my heart and introducing me to the spirit world, the God Force. For teaching me the soul in the dance!

15662448R00082

Made in the USA
Lexington, KY
10 June 2012